Discover

Sout.. ...
Western Australia

A Hema Outdoor Guide

by Denis O'Byrne

Your guide to a complete South West WA experience

Discover South West WA

This is the second in a series of outdoor guides, published by Hema Maps Pty Ltd and originated by Rob van Driesum. The guides complement the maps that Hema produces, with a focus on outdoor activities.

The Author of this Book

Denis O'Byrne is a freelance journalist and writer currently living in Darwin. He has been writing about travel and the outdoors for over 25 years, and his work has appeared in numerous publications including the national 4WD magazine *Overlander* and various Lonely Planet guides.

Credits and Thanks

Many people willingly provided Denis with assistance and advice during the preparation of this guide and he's very grateful to them all. Those whom he particularly would like to mention are: Terry Bolland (Canoeing Down Under); Geoff Harnett (CALM Stirling Range National Park); Chris Goodsell (CALM Walpole); Ian Hughes (CALM Stokes National Park); David Meehan (CALM Pemberton); Jason Nelthorpe (Nannup Visitor Centre); Pam Riordan (Inspiration Outdoors); Tracey Robins (CALM Calgardup Cave); Allan Rose (CALM Cape Arid National Park); Jo Smith (Esperance Visitor Centre); Pam Watts (Bunbury Visitor Centre); and Peter Wilkins (CALM Fitzgerald River National Park).

Last but by no means least, Snow & Glad Hansen, Pauline Hansen, Les & Lesley Mitting and Phil & Kerry Smyth generously allowed him to take over their dining room tables and/or spare bedrooms.

Change is Certain

The information presented in this book is always subject to change. Roads change, rules and policies are amended, and new facilities and services spring up while existing ones go out of business. Quoted schedules, prices and contact details were correct at the time of research, but you should always check with operators to avoid disappointment.

This book can only be a guide and should not be taken as gospel. The best advice is to keep an open mind and talk to others as you explore this beautiful corner of Australia – it's all part of the adventure.

Please Tell Us

We welcome and appreciate all your comments and any information that helps us improve and update future editions of this book. Please write to Hema Maps Pty Ltd, PO Box 4365, Eight Mile Plains, Qld 4113, Australia.

Published by

Hema Maps Pty Ltd
PO Box 4365
Eight Mile Plains, Qld 4113
Australia
✆ (07) 3340 0000
Fax (07) 3340 0099
manager@hemamaps.com.au
www.hemamaps.com
1st edition – July 2004
ISBN 1-86500-278-X

Photographs
Front cover:
Greens Pool, Tree Top Walk, Beach fishing, photos by Rob Boegheim;
Red Kangaroo Paw, photo by Rob van Driesum

Back cover:
Organ Pipes in Jewel Cave, photo by Rob van Driesum

Publisher: Rob Boegheim
Managing Editor: Rob van Driesum
Assistant Editor: Natalie Wilson
Author: Denis O'Byrne
Cartographer: Ray Martin
Designers: Wendy Ealey, Debbie Winfield
Cover/Title Page Design: Debbie Winfield

Contents

Contents

Introduction

The South West of Western Australia is a happy hunting ground for outdoor pursuits, and if you're expecting something different and exciting you won't be disappointed.

Several qualities other than isolation set the South West apart from the rest of Australia. First there are its native forests – magical places dominated by karri, one of the world's tallest hardwoods. Next, wildflowers. It doesn't happen every year, but given the right combination of temperature and rainfall the springtime displays will take your breath away. Also outstanding is the unique wildlife, with a number of opportunities to see rare mammals in the wild and swim with dolphins. As for the coast, there are so many dazzling surf beaches that you'll soon run out of superlatives.

There are no snowfields in the South West, but otherwise there is an excellent range of air, land and water-based pursuits. In fact, few parts of Australia have so much potential packed into such a small area. The list of things to do – and places to do them in – is as long as your arm. Bird-watching, bushwalking, canoeing, cycling, fishing, four-wheel driving, scuba diving, surfing, swimming, whale-watching, windsurfing and yachting are all popular. Aboriginal culture tours give a fascinating insight into the ancient traditions of the Nyoongar people, the South West's original inhabitants. For the more adventurous, there are also great opportunities for abseiling, adventure caving, hang-gliding, hot-air ballooning, paragliding, rock climbing, horse riding and white-water rafting.

You'll notice too that we've included a look at the region's wineries. While enjoyment of the fruits of Bacchus is not necessarily an outdoor activity in itself, a celebratory drop of local red or white after completing any of the pursuits mentioned certainly forms part of the overall experience.

Finally, we don't claim that this book lists every outdoor pursuit and every possible venue. Our hope is that it'll serve to point you in the right direction when you're indulging in an outdoor holiday in this truly remarkable corner of Australia. ■

Kings Park

Rottnest Island

Wineries

Pinnacles

Flora

Karri Forests

Margaret River Region

Wave Rock

Chapter One

Backgrounds

Highlights

The South West has so many different attractions for lovers of the outdoors that it's hard to imagine anyone not finding something to enthral them. Even typical Aussie blokes, who might feel more at home conquering a 4WD track or fishing with a few mates, find themselves being captivated by the region's tall karri forests and colourful displays of spring wildflowers. The following list of highlights is pretty subjective and by no means exhaustive, but hopefully it'll give you an idea of what to expect. They're listed in the order in which they're described in this book:

- **Kings Park.** Enjoy a picnic, view stunning cityscapes, discover myriad local plants, or explore a bushland trail all of this and more right in the centre of Perth.
- **Rottnest Island.** Enjoy a variety of water sports, laze on a secluded beach or meet a quokka on Perth's wonderful holiday isle.
- **Winery Tours.** Take time out for a discovery tour of one (or two) of the emerging and established wine regions that lie scattered between Perth and Albany.
- **Munda Biddi Trail.** When completed (hopefully by 2006) this 900km mountain bike route through national parks and state forests will connect Mundaring (near Perth) to Albany. Stage One between Mundaring and Collie (300km) opened in mid-2004.
- **Wildflowers.** It's already been said – unbelievable. From Cervantes around to Esperance and beyond, the coastal heathland can be a blooming miracle in spring.
- **Pinnacles Desert.** Experience the eerie landscape of the Pinnacles Desert in Nambung National Park. You'll soon see why early Dutch mariners thought it was a ruined city.

- **Dolphin Discoveries.** Meet the friendly wild dolphins that come in daily to Bunbury's Dolphin Discovery Centre on Koombana Bay.
- **Busselton Jetty.** Discover a huge and fascinating diversity of small fish, crustaceans, corals and other marine life from the comfort of an underwater observation chamber.
- **Margaret River Region.** Surfers who happen to worship Bacchus will think they've arrived in paradise. Several world-class breaks can be found along the coast here, while over 80 wineries pump out a variety of excellent wines.
- **Cape-to-Cape Track.** This 135km coastal walk near Margaret River is one stunning view after another. Go the whole way on a single trek, or spend a day discovering one of the track's five sections.
- **Nannup.** Inspect an open garden, go on a forest walk or canoeing trip, or step back in time on a stroll along the main street of this quaint little timber town.
- **Karri Forests.** The virgin karri forests around Pemberton are special places whose spirit touches all who visit them. Climb to the top of a fire lookout tree, or simply relax and enjoy the cathedral-calm atmosphere created by these magnificent giants.
- **Tree Top Walk.** Still in the tall timber, the elevated walkway through the forest canopy near Nornalup is a 'must do'. The neighbouring 'Ancient Empire' is equally impressive.
- **Whale-Watching.** Be enthralled by the antics of humpback and southern right whales on their annual breeding and calving migrations along the South West coast.
- **Whale World Museum.** Learn about whales and the whaling industry on a visit

to this fascinating museum, set in an old whaling station near Albany.

- **Stirling Range.** The South West's nearest thing to mountainous country, the rugged Stirling Range rises dramatically from the surrounding wheat paddocks to form one of the state's most important botanical areas. Bluff Knoll, the highest point, is a magnet for climbers and walkers.
- **Bibbulmun Track.** This 963km footpath links Perth to Albany and forms one of Australia's great walks. Allow eight weeks to explore it end to end.
- **Cape Le Grand**. It's easy to run out of superlatives when describing the coastal scenery of this national park east of Esperance. Wharton's Beach, at the park's eastern end, must be one of the state's most beautiful stretches of sand – and there's not even a beach shack to mar the view.
- **Dryandra Woodland.** Attractive wandoo woodlands and a chance to observe some of Australia's endangered mammal species are major draws in this wheatbelt reserve.
- **Wave Rock.** Stand under one of Australia's most unusual landforms and imagine that it's a huge breaker about to come crashing down on your head.

Orientation

When local tourism people refer to the South West of Western Australia they often mean a small region south of Perth. A geographer, if asked to define the South West, would almost certainly take a broader view. Naturalists certainly do – the South West Botanical Province is delineated by a line drawn roughly between Shark Bay and Esperance.

This guide is largely restricted to a broad belt extending inland up to 150km along the coast from Nambung National Park in the north to beyond Esperance in the east. The topography here is generally flat to undulating, with significantly hilly areas confined to the Darling Range, which extends about 300km from north of Perth to east of Bunbury, and the Stirling and Porongurup ranges near Albany. Native forests form a broad arc paralleling the coast from Perth to Denmark (near Albany). Elsewhere the native vegetation has largely been cleared for agricultural development.

The South West includes the state capital, Perth, and numerous mainly small farming and forestry centres. The only country towns of significant size outside Perth are Mandurah (pop 44,000), Albany (29,000) and Bunbury (28,000). Albany is about 400km southeast of Perth, while Mandurah and Bunbury are 75 and 160km south respectively.

History

Mariners landing on the South West coast hundreds of years ago found a land that was already inhabited. These people lived in family groups that spoke dialects of a common language and referred to themselves as Nyoongar. While they did not build lasting monuments, there is a wealth of more subtle evidence of their long occupancy. For example, bone and stone tools found at a site near Cape Leeuwin have been dated at 31,000 years before present. At Swan Bridge, near Perth, are the remains of a campfire that burned 39,500 years ago.

European Explorers

The identity of the first 'foreigners' to sight these shores is shrouded in mystery. Were they Dutch, Chinese, Portuguese or some other nationality? Whichever, the first recorded visitors were hardy Dutch mariners in the *Leeuwin*. In 1622, while on a voyage from Holland to the East Indies, they sighted the continent's southwestern tip and named it "'t Landt van der Leeuwin" (the Land of the Lioness). They were followed by the *Gulden Zeepaardt* under Francois Thijssen who, in 1627, charted the south coast from Cape Leeuwin to Ceduna, in South Australia. Seventy years later Willem de Vlamingh landed near Perth while searching for survivors from a missing ship. During his brief visit de Vlamingh found an Aboriginal camp, but no sign of its occupants, and named Rottnest Island and the Swan River.

Almost a hundred years passed before the next explorers arrived on the scene. In 1791 George Vancouver sailed into King George Sound (where Albany now stands) and formally claimed the land for Britain. The numerous French place names along the coast south of Bunbury relate to visits by French scientific expeditions under the command of Bruni D'Entrecasteaux (1792) and Nicolas Baudin

(1802). Matthew Flinders visited the south coast in 1801-02 on his way to chart the unknown coastline further east.

European Settlers

Afraid that the French would beat them to it, the British established a military outpost at King George Sound in 1826. This was followed three years later by the Swan River colony (now Perth). As happened in many other parts of Australia, relations with the Aboriginal people were friendly at first, but mutual misunderstandings and competing demands for resources soon led to trouble. Nyoongar leaders began a doomed resistance that was crushed at the so-called Battle of Pinjarra in 1834.

Generous land grants brought settlers flocking to the new colony, yet its birth was anything but easy. The soil was infertile and there was an extreme labour shortage – in 1848 the population of over 40,000 included just a thousand labourers. The latter problem was largely overcome by the importation of almost 10,000 convicts from England between 1850 and 1868.

Development & 'Separateness'

Wheat and wool were the mainstays of the economy, but the harsh, dry interior meant that population growth and economic development were slow. It took a series of rich gold strikes in the 1880s to put the colony on its feet and allow it to be granted responsible government in 1890.

Isolation from the rest of Australia has always given Western Australians a sense of separateness, and when the referendum on federation came there was a push for the colony to go its own way. However, the thousands of diggers from eastern Australia then working on the goldfields ensured a 'yes' vote.

By the time of the Great Depression the wealth generated by gold had dissipated and the state's economy was once again dependent on agriculture. Commodity prices crashed as a result of the Depression and the economy collapsed in the early 1930s. Many Western Australians felt that the Federal Government was ignoring their plight and this fanned the flames of secession. Indeed, feelings ran so high that when a referendum on the subject was held in 1933 electors voted almost two to one to leave the Commonwealth. The result was declared invalid for legal reasons and the next step was never taken.

The state economy remained in the doldrums until after WWII, when the Federal Government's immigration policy resulted in a dramatic increase in the population. These new immigrants, most of whom were British, included Alan Bond in their ranks. The spectacular rise of Bond and other high-flying business entrepreneurs in the 1970s and '80s created the illusion that Western Australia was a promised land where anyone could get rich. This myth was shattered by the stock-market crash of 1987.

Today Western Australia is the nation's richest state per capita thanks to its vast mineral wealth. Many Western Australians resent the fact that their state contributes a disproportionate amount of the nation's wealth. This enhances the feeling of separateness that is often just beneath the surface.

Geology & Landforms

The early geological history of the South West is a violent tale of collision and rupture as new continents were created, then torn apart. The first of these landmasses was the Yilgarn Craton, which drifted around for 1000 million years or more until it bumped into the Pilbara Craton to form the West Australian Craton.

About 1300 million years ago (mya) this vast continent collided with the Mawson Craton along what is now the south coast. A huge mountain range was thrust up, the upheaval creating the igneous and metamorphic rocks that help make the Porongurup Range and the coast from Point D'Entrecasteaux to Cape Arid such a spectacular sight.

A similar range was formed along the western edge of the Yilgarn Craton about 1100 mya when another continent collided with it. (Most of its rocks now lie buried deep beneath the Swan Coastal Plain, which extends from

Geraldton to Dunsborough.) The western edge of this new range was marked by the Darling Fault, a major structure that can be traced for 1000km from near Point D'Entrecasteaux to east of Shark Bay. Parts of the Yilgarn Craton were uplifted along the fault to form the ancestral Darling Range.

By now the continent of Gondwana had been formed. India tore itself away about 135 mya, creating a rupture in the crust that allowed lava to escape. A legacy of that period is the dramatic basalt cliffs at Black Point in D'Entrecasteaux National Park. The metamorphic rocks that underlie the limestone of the Leeuwin-Naturaliste Ridge are another result of the forces generated by Gondwana's break-up.

Following India's departure came periodic changes in sea level and the development of the present drainage system. About 40 mya most of the South West was inundated by a shallow sea whose floor became covered by a thick layer of sponge skeletons. This material consolidated into a soft rock called spongelike that now forms colourful gorges in the Fitzgerald River National Park.

The sea level has changed dramatically over the past two million years as the polar ice caps have expanded and contracted. Sand dunes and beaches deposited at a time when the sea level was 130m lower than now became the limestone that forms Rottnest Island and the spectacular sea cliffs in D'Entrecasteaux National Park. The caves of Yanchep and Leeuwin-Naturaliste national parks were created in this soft rock.

About 6500 years ago the sea level rose to its present height. Flooded valleys formed the present estuaries and Rottnest Island became separated from the mainland.

Flora & Fauna

Flora

Long isolation from the plants of southeastern Australia has resulted in the South West becoming one of the world's richest and most diverse botanical provinces – a staggering 75% of its 7000 species of flowering plants are found nowhere else. This unique flora includes forest giants such as karri and marri, the kangaroo paw, wax flower, one-sided bottlebrush, *Kingia* and *Dryandra*, all of which evolved here. Others, such as *Darwinia* (mountain bells), *Gastrolobium* (poison pea), featherflowers, and trigger plants, appeared before the region became isolated, but developed here more than elsewhere in Australia's temperate zone.

Sadly, however, the region's rich biodiversity is being seriously threatened by a veritable host of factors including too-frequent fires, land clearing, grazing pressure, rising groundwater, increasing salinity, weed invasion, climate change and the spread of dieback (see p14). Many threatened plant species are likely to become extinct over the next half-century even if everything possible is done to stem the onslaught. Unfortunately there are no quick fixes for over 150 years of ignorance and mismanagement.

Trees of the Tall Forests

The loamy soils of the South West's wetter parts are known for their forests of karri and tingle. Jarrah is most common on the drier lateritic country north of the Blackwood River, while tuart forests are confined to the limestone soils of the Swan Coastal Plain. These tall species dominate a rich diversity of understorey plants such as acacias, she-oaks,

ROB VAN DRIESUM

Sunsets in the South West are awesome

One-sided bottlebrush

The Mangles kangaroo paw is the floral emblem of WA

The tall kangaroo paw thrives in swampy areas

The brilliant red kangaroo paw grows in white sand near the coast from Albany eastwards, but is also common in the Stirling Range

banksias, peppermint, paperbarks and various eucalypts. The forests have been heavily logged, but old-growth stands still survive within national parks.

Karri *(Eucalyptus diversicolor)* grows to 90m high and is one of the world's tallest hardwoods. It is identified by its long, straight trunk and smooth bark, which is shed in summer resulting in the tree having a multi-hued appearance. Karri grows mainly between Nannup, Manjimup and Denmark and is an important structural hardwood. In recent years a large percentage of the karri forest has been felled for woodchips. The remaining karri forest covers around 2000ha, of which nearly 90% is on land managed by the WA government's Department of Conservation & Land Management (CALM).

Although not quite as tall as karri, **red tingle** *(Eucalyptus jacksonii)* is by far the most impressive eucalypt in terms of girth. Its huge, buttressed trunk, which can have a circumference exceeding 20m, is often hollowed out as a result of being burned in forest fires. Red tingle is confined to the lower catchments of the Bow, Deep and Frankland rivers. The so-called Ancient Empire is an awe-inspiring group of red tingles adjacent to the Tree Top Walk near Nornalup.

Karri forest

Jarrah *(Eucalyptus marginata)* reaches 40m in height – a real surprise considering the infertility of the soil on which it grows. Mature specimens have long, thick, straight trunks topped by a tangle of branches; the species can be identified by its fibrous bark, which is grey/brown and has vertical grooves. Jarrah timber is highly prized both for its appearance (it varies in colour from rich red/brown to soft pink and has an attractive, dense grain), strength and durability. Indeed, jarrah timber is so durable that it was widely used as dock piles and railway sleepers, not to mention paving for the streets of London. The original jarrah forest was almost destroyed by reckless logging and much of what remains is under threat from disease and strip mining – jarrah has the misfortune to grow on soil that is rich in bauxite. CALM manages about 1.4 million ha of jarrah forest, most of it regrowth.

Reaching a maximum 60m in height, **marri** *(Corymbia calophylla)* is one of the South West's most common and widespread forest species. It has a dark, flaky bark and often oozes dark red sap from its trunk. **Tuart** *(Eucalyptus gomphocephala)* is much more restricted, being found in isolated stands between Jurien Bay and Busselton; over 35% of the original tuart forest has been cleared for agriculture and the only substantial remnants are in national parks. Tuart grows to 40m high and has roughish, grey bark. It is often associated with

peppermint *(Agonis flexuosa)*, which is readily identified by the smell of peppermint exuded by freshly crushed leaves.

Another interesting forest tree is the **red-flowering gum** *(Corymbia ficifolia)*, a straggly species that is transformed in summer by masses of flowers that vary from scarlet through to pale pink. The parasitic **Christmas tree** *(Nuytsia floribunda)*, also a summer bloomer, is easily identified from its vivid orange flowers. It is widespread throughout the region.

Named after the famous early botanist, banksias are widespread in the South West forests and other vegetation types. They are readily identified by their domed or cylindrical flower spikes – a rich source of nectar for many mammals, birds and insects. A common understorey species of the jarrah forest, **bull banksia** *(Banksia grandis)* grows to 10m and has huge, yellow flower cones up to 40cm long. Sadly, this genus is particularly susceptible to dieback.

Woodlands

Woodlands dominated by eucalypts and acacias are found on the heavier clay-loam soils to the north and east of the tall forests. **Raspberry jam** *(Acacia acuminata)* is common on red loam, often in association with **York gum** *(Eucalyptus laxophleba)* and **wandoo** *(Eucalyptus wandoo)*. Much of these woodlands have been cleared for agriculture, but a few significant remnants can still be seen in conservation areas like Dryandra.

The karri she-oak only grows to 15m and has a thick, corky bark

ROB VAN DRIESUM

ESPERANCE REGION TOURISM ASSOCIATION

The stunning Christmas tree, with its bright orange blossoms, is actually a parasitic mistletoe – the only mistletoe that grows as a tree

Bull banksia

Baxter's banksia with its triangular leaves is popular in the cut flower industry. The velvet, red seed cones are also attractive

Tassel shrub, a member of the southern heath family (Epacridaceae)

ROB VANDRIESUM

Heath

Large areas of the South West are covered by stunted, heath-like vegetation called **Kwongan**. These communities, which are commonly associated with taller shrubs such as banksia and mallee, are usually found on the poorest of soils (deep sands and shallow sand over laterite) in the 250-400mm-rainfall belt. Yet ironically, Kwongan is one of the world's most diverse types of vegetation, comparable in richness to tropical rainforests. Except in spring, when a good year sees it transformed by an explosion of colourful wildflowers, the heath can seem drab and monotonous and you'll wonder what the fuss is about. However, a closer inspection can reveal dozens of species growing in a few square metres, with members of the *Epacridaceae*, *Fabaceae*, *Myrtaceae*, and *Proteaceae* families being particularly dominant.

The most interesting assemblage of plants, some of which are truly bizarre, occurs in Fitzgerald River National Park. Around 1900 species are found here, including 75 endemics and 250 rare or restricted species.

Orchids

Australia has around 800 species of terrestrial orchids, of which 350 are found in the South West. They occur in a variety of habitats including heaths, seasonal swamps, mountain peaks and tall forests. Each of these habitats has its own suite of species.

The variety inherent in orchid flowers seems endless. Some, such as the **pink enamel orchids** *(Elythranthera emarginata)* of wandoo woodlands, are noted for their rich colour. The scented **sun orchid** *(Thelymitra macrophylla)*

Backgrounds

has large, fragrant flowers whose colour ranges from mauve to white. **Blue ladies** (*T. crinita*) and also the strikingly marked **Queen of Sheba** (*T. variegata*) are gems of the jarrah forest.

Some orchids form large colonies of hundreds if not thousands of plants in which spectacular massed flowerings can occur. These include **pink fairies** (*Caladinia latifolia*), the **cowslip orchid** (*C. flava flava*) and the lemon-scented **sun orchid** (*Thelymitra antennifera*); its fragrance can be detected some distance away.

Other species are noted for their exquisite forms, stunning examples being the **butterfly orchid** (*Caladenia lobata*), the white **spider orchid** (*C. longicauda*) and the **hare orchid** (*Leporella fimbriata*). All three are found in a variety of habitats. There is also the weird and wonderful, such as **helmet orchids** (*Chorybas*), the **slipper orchid** (*Cryptostylis ovata*), **hammer orchids** (*Drakeae*) and the **rabbit orchid** (*Leptoceras menziesii*).

Fauna

Land Mammals

The South West is home to 47 species of non-marine mammals, eight of which are bats and 11 of which are classed as vulnerable to extinction. They range in size from mouse-sized creatures like the **honey possum** (*Tarsipes rostratus*), **long-tailed dunnart** (*Sminthopsis dolichura*), **western pygmy-possum** (*Cercartetus conncinus*) and **ash-grey mouse** (*Pseudomys*

ESPERANCE REGION TOURISM ASSOCIATION

The Creeping Scourge

As you travel around the jarrah forests and banksia woodlands of the South West you'll notice patches of dead trees and other plants that appear to be succumbing to drought. The likely culprit is *Phytophthora cinnamomi*, an introduced, microscopic, water-borne fungus that is cutting a swathe of death through the region's native vegetation.

Phytophthora cinnamomi is a parasite that infects the feeder roots of susceptible plants, causing the roots to die and thus cutting off the plant's water supply. It was probably brought in early in the last century and is now found from 300km north of Perth to east of Esperance. As many as 1000 species are at risk; some, such as banksias and dryandras, succumb very quickly once infected while others, such as jarrah, are more resistant and may survive small infections.

The fungus requires moisture to spread naturally. Its spores are carried down slope by rainwater run-off and groundwater, as a result of which damp, low-lying areas become heavily infected. What is worse, however, is the artificial spread of the fungus. Muddy soil containing the spores can collect in tyre treads, vehicle underbodies and on walkers' footwear and can then be transported over long distances to healthy areas. When the infected mud or soil drops off, the fungus immediately begins to colonise the new area.

Once *Phytophthora cinnamomi* becomes established it is impossible to eradicate, so control efforts are directed at stopping its spread. Roads and tracks in some national parks and state forests have been closed to protect dieback-free areas of high conservation value. Bushwalkers are urged to clean their footwear (including the soles) immediately at the completion of any walk through a dieback-infected area. 'Boot-cleaning' stations consisting of trays of water and brushes are often provided for this purpose. Please use them.

albocinereus) to the **western grey kangaroo** *(Macropus fuliginosus)*. Most, however, are smaller than a rabbit. Following are some of the more interesting ones.

To anyone who has visited Rottnest Island, one of the region's most familiar mammals is the **quokka** *(Setonix brachyurus)*. Once common and widespread, this rabbit-sized species is now restricted on the mainland to isolated pockets of dense vegetation near swamps and streams. At Two Peoples Bay, near Albany, it shares this habitat with the critically endangered **Gilbert's potoroo** *(Potorous tridactylus gilbertii)*, which was dramatically rediscovered here in 1994 – it had not been recorded anywhere since the 1870s. Also once presumed extinct, the **dibbler** *(Parantechinus apicalis)* was found alive and well in the same area in 1967. Colonies of these attractive, rat-sized animals have since been discovered elsewhere.

One of the most photogenic of all the region's mammals, the **chuditch** *(Dasyurus geoffroii)* was once persecuted as a raider of chook pens. It too once had a much wider range, but is now found only in the South West where it mainly occurs in jarrah forests. The chuditch, which is about the size of a small cat, is easily identifiable by its white-spotted, brown coat. It's sometimes caught raiding rubbish bins in picnic and camping areas.

The **quenda** *(Isoodon obesulus)* may also be seen searching for food scraps in recreation areas, usually at dawn and dusk. These rabbit-sized members of the bandicoot family have large hindquarters and a long, pointed snout.

A depressingly large percentage of local mammals is either threatened or endangered, with few species being more at risk than the **red-tailed phascogale** *(Phascogale calura)*. This small, elusive animal is an extremely good climber and spends most of its time in trees, as does its much more common cousin, the **brush-tailed phascogale** *(P. tapoatafa)*. Curiously, male phascogales die soon after doing their bit in a short but frantic breeding season.

Marine Mammals

Once hunted to the edge of extinction, and still regarded as endangered, **humpback whales** *(Megaptera novaeangliae)* and **southern right whales** *(Eubalaena australis)* are a magnificent feature of the South West coast between May and December. Early in this period they leave their feeding grounds in the Southern Ocean and migrate northwards to breed and calve in warmer coastal waters, before returning in late spring.

Both species have been fully protected for many years, but the recovery of their decimated populations isn't going to happen overnight. It's estimated that worldwide only a few thousand humpbacks and southern rights were left at the cessation of hunting. The population of southern rights along the Australian coast still only numbers in the hundreds. At their slow rate of breeding (one calf every three years) it will be a long time yet before these huge but gentle creatures will be seen in anything like their former numbers.

Sperm whales *(Physeter macrocephalus)* are inhabitants of deep oceans throughout the world and are often found relatively close to the mainland near Albany. Despite being hunted for over 300 years and having an extremely low birth rate – calves are born at intervals of between three and 15 years – the species remains fairly numerous. Females spend their lives in family groups of 10-20 animals, while the males live in bachelor pods. Sperm whales dive to depths of 2800m or more in search of squid, their favoured food.

A number of other whale species inhabit the waters off the South West coast, but are seldom seen near the shore. **Scamperdown whales** *(Mesoplodon bowdoini)*, **strap-toothed whales** *(Mesoplodon layardii)*, **long-finned pilot whales** *(Globicephala melas)* and **false killer whales** *(Pseudorca crassidens)* strand themselves fairly frequently – several mass strandings of false killer whales have occurred near Augusta. **Killer whales** *(Orcinus orca)* are usually seen following the humpbacks along the coast.

See also Whale-Watching p37 for more about whales.

The most common marine mammal in South Western coastal waters is the **bottlenose dolphin** *(Tursiops truncates)*. Found all over the world, it is often seen in estuaries and close to shore along beaches and reefs. They are highly social animals and occupy defined home territories. See Swimming with Marine Mammals pp36-37.

Australian sea lions *(Neophoca cinerea)* occur on offshore islands right around the South West coast. Endemic to Western

Back from the Brink

The first British explorers and settlers were captivated by the huge variety of small to medium-sized mammals they found inhabiting the South West bush. Yet by the 1950s most of these animals had vanished from agricultural areas and were well on the way to extinction. The reasons for this environmental disaster included loss of habitat, introduction of foxes and feral cats, competition from introduced grazing animals, and changes in fire regimes.

The larger mammals – western grey kangaroos *(Macropus fuliginosus)*, western brush wallabies *(Macropus irma)*, brush-tailed possums *(Trichosurus vulpecular)* and echidnas *(Tachyglossus aculeatus)* – remained fairly common. However, some medium-sized species had disappeared forever, while others hung on in small isolated areas, such as offshore islands, where foxes and rabbits are scarce.

Prior to the 1970s, feral rabbit numbers in the South West were controlled by laying baits poisoned with 1080. "Ten-eighty" is the synthetic version of sodium fluoroacetate, a naturally occurring compound found in plants of the genus *Gastrolobium*. The genus is well represented in the South West, where it is widespread. Over millions of years the local wildlife has developed immunity to sodium flouroacetate, but it's deadly to newcomers like rabbits and foxes.

In the 1970s rabbit fleas were introduced to spread the myxoma virus, and 1080 poisoning was phased out. An unwelcome side-effect of this was that foxes – which had been eating the poisoned rabbits, with fatal consequences for them – now began to rapidly increase. Soon the South West's remaining native mammal populations were falling to new lows.

In the early 1980s wildlife researchers began to study what the effects on native animals would be if foxes were poisoned with 1080. The result was a dramatic increase in sightings of numbats *(Myrmecobius fasciatus)*, woylies *(Bettongia penicillata)*, possums and tammar wallabies *(Macropus eugenii)*. These experiments were the beginning of CALM's ongoing predator control and reintroduction programme, known as Western Shield, which began in 1996.

The success of Western Shield has made it possible to reintroduce 16 native mammal species to a number of conservation areas from which they had previously disappeared. Many of the translocated animals were bred at Dryandra, while others were transferred from recovering wild populations. In a stunning reversal of previous trends, the programme has enabled the quenda, tammar wallaby and woylie to be removed from the list of WA's threatened fauna. The status of the chuditch, currently vulnerable, is being reviewed as its situation has improved markedly in recent years. Hopefully more will soon follow.

Australian and South Australian waters, this species has a total population of 9-12,000 animals, making it one of the world's rarest sea lions. **New Zealand fur seals** *(Arctocephalus forsteri)* have a much wider range, but in WA are restricted to islands off the southern coast. Like whales, hunting in the 18th and 19th centuries decimated the populations of both these species.

Birds

Upwards of 250 species, not including migratory waders and sea birds, are regularly recorded in the South West. However, unlike the region's flora, endemism among the bird fauna is low compared with structurally similar habitats in south eastern Australia – the

Short-billed black cockatoos like to feed on banksias

entire region has just 11 endemic species as well as several endemic subspecies. The low diversity of birds in forested areas is partly a result of that ecosystem's poor productivity. It also reflects the likely extinctions that took place during periods of extreme aridity in Pleistocene times, when forest habitats shrank dramatically.

Forest endemics include the **red-eared firetail** *(Stagonopleura oculata)*, **western thornbill** *(Acanthiza inornata)*, **red-winged fairy wren** *(Malurus elegans)* and **white-breasted robin** *(Eopsaltria georgiana)*. The region's four endemic cockatoos and parrots are more widespread, although the **short-billed (Carnaby's) black-cockatoo** *(Calyptorhynchus latirostris)* and **long-billed (Baudin's) black-cockatoo** *(C. baudinii)* are both considered endangered as a result of habitat loss. The **western rosella** *(Platycerus icterotis)* and **red-capped parrot** *(Purpureicephalus spurius)* are common and colourful denizens of forest and woodland areas.

The region's most famous endemic is the **noisy scrub-bird** *(Atrichornis clamosus)*, a small, elusive songster restricted to dense scrub along drainage lines at two locations near Albany. It was presumed extinct until 'rediscovered' in 1961. The **western spinebill** *(Acanthorhynchus superciliosus)* is a common species of woodlands and heaths, but the **western bristle-bird** *(Dasyornis longirostris)*, also found in heaths, is endangered.

While several endemic species and subspecies are threatened or endangered, as far as is known only one – the western subspecies of the rufous bristle-bird *(Dasyornis broadbenti litoralis)* – has become extinct since white settlement. It was last sighted in 1906.

For more on birds, see pp27-28. ■

Young kookaburra

Wind farm near Esperance

ROB BOEGHEIM

The South West Coast is often spectacular

Information Sources

State & Local Tourist Offices

The Western Australian Tourist Commission (WATC, www.westernaustralia.net) has its visitor information centre and travel agency on the corner of Forrest Place and Wellington St, Perth. The centre is open daily and can be contacted on ✆ 1300 361 351 – if required, the consultant will put you through to a travel expert in your area of interest.

See the later regional chapters for contact details of local tourist offices.

CALM Offices

The Department of Conservation & Land Management (CALM, www.naturebase.net) manages all national parks, nature reserves, marine parks and state forests. The state operational headquarters (✆ 08 9334 0333) is at 17 Dick Perry Ave, Kensington 6151; its regional offices are at:

- **Swan Region (Perth)** – 20 Dick Perry Ave, Kensington 6151 (✆ 08 9368 4399)
- **South West Region** – cnr South West Hwy & Dodson St, Bunbury 6230 (✆ 08 9725 4300)
- **Southern Forest Region** – Brain St, Manjimup 6258 (✆ 08 9771 7988)
- **South Coast Region** -120 Albany Hwy, Albany 6330 (✆ 08 9842 4500)
- **Wheatbelt Region** – 7 Wald St, Narrogin 6312 (✆ 08 9881 1444)

CALM Outdoors (✆ 08 9399 9745) at 40 Jull St, Armadale, is an information centre where you'll find a wide range of publications such as topographic maps, activity guides, reference books, walks brochures and fact sheets.

Other Useful Sources

Backpacker hostels and speciality outdoor shops such as Mainpeak, Mountain Designs and Snowgum can be good alternative sources of information on outdoor activities.

Books & Magazines

A number of guides deal with specific activities (e.g. fishing, walking, rock climbing) and these are listed in the What to Do chapter. However, useful references of a general nature relevant to planning a trip to the South West are in short supply. Those worth getting hold of include:

- Annear, Rod et al, 1999, *Wild Places Quiet Places*, Department of Conservation & Land Management, Kensington WA – gives a reasonably comprehensive introduction to the South West's national parks and major reserves; includes a lot of information on ancillary matters such as acting responsibly in the bush.
- Nevill, Simon, 2000, *Travellers Guide to the Parks & Reserves of Western Australia*, Simon Nevill Publications, South Fremantle WA – a well-researched book covering over 100 conservation areas throughout the state, with sections on general topics such as planning and preparation.
- Ashworth, Egger, Mattinson & Turner, 2004, *Western Australia*, Lonely Planet Publications, Footscray Vic – a useful general reference with a lot of information on the South West.
- *Landscope*, Department of Conservation & Land Management, Kensington WA a glossy quarterly magazine dealing with natural history, national parks and conservation issues. You'll find back copies in public libraries.

- *Scoop Traveller*, Concept Reality Media Group, Subiaco WA – another home-grown glossy quarterly, this magazine specialises in travel stories on Western Australia.

Maps

Most of the maps in the back of this book come from Hema's *South West Western Australia* map, while coverage of the Esperance region comes from Hema's overall *Western Australia* map. They should suffice for most car drivers. Serious four-wheel drivers, cyclists or bushwalkers, however, may wish to refer to the more detailed, limited-area Streetsmart and/or CALM maps discussed below.

Hema's *South West Western Australia* covers the region at a scale of 1:750,000. The reverse side is given over to descriptions of towns and regional highlights. Hema's *Perth and Region Handy Map* is similar but replaces the descriptions of towns and highlights with a 1:80,000 map of Perth and its suburbs.

Streetsmart (an arm of the Department of Land Information, DLI) produces a range of touring maps that provide excellent coverage of limited areas. These include the *Southern Forests* and *Lower Great Southern*, both at 1:175,000, and the *South West Corner* at 1:125,000. All contain plenty of useful information as well as town and regional maps.

CALM has mapped the national parks and state forests at 1:50,000, while DLI (or its previous incarnation, DOLA) has mapped the coastal strip from the Moore River to Augusta at 1:25,000. These maps are available from Map World at 900 Hay St, Perth. Outside Perth, try the Chart & Map Shop, 14 Collie St, Fremantle; Albany Map Centre, 126 York St, Albany; and CALM offices and tourist centres.

When to Go

Any time is a good time to be in the South West it all depends on what it is that you want to do. The following information may help.

Climate

The South West has a Mediterranean climate of hot, dry summers and cool, wet winters, with maritime influences near the coast. In inland areas maximum temperatures frequently rise above 35 degrees in summer, while winter minimums often fall below zero. Albany is usually a few degrees cooler than Perth, which is ideal in summer – perhaps less so in winter. Storms often lash the southern coast during winter. On the other hand, the atmosphere produced by a mist over the karri forests makes winter a special time to visit these areas.

Crowds

Things can go a little crazy during Easter and WA school holiday periods. In summer, like anywhere else, local folk flock to the coast like migrating birds – late December to late January is the main crowd 'danger' period. In September/October the wildflowers lure hordes of visitors – many from interstate –

Moonrise

into the countryside. Obviously it would be wise to book accommodation well in advance if you're intending to visit these areas during their busy times.

National Park Passes

Entry to many of the South West's national parks is subject to a fee. There are several passes available, and you can purchase them at CALM offices, park entry points and selected tourist centres and shops. Ring © 08 9334 0333 to get the location of your nearest outlet.

In the following list, "vehicle" means a vehicle that can legally seat up to eight people. For most visitors, a Holiday Pass is the best option:

- **Day Pass** – valid for one day only and covers entry to as many parks as you can visit in that time. Costs $9 per vehicle (motorcycles and concession holders $3).
- **Holiday Pass** – covers entry to all parks for up to four weeks. Costs $22.50 per vehicle.
- **Annual Local Park Pass** – allows unlimited entry to one park (or group of local parks) for a period of one year. Costs $17 per vehicle.
- **All Parks Annual Pass** – allows unlimited entry to all parks in Western Australia for a year. Costs $51 per vehicle.
- **Gold Star Pass** – includes the All Parks Annual Pass and a 12-month subscription to Landscope magazine. Costs $73 per vehicle.

ROB BOEGHEIM

Hikers should be prepared for sudden changes in the weather, as indicated by this 'sun shower' at Bluff Knoll in the Stirling Range

Communications

Telephone STD Code

The STD code for Western Australia is 08.

Internet Access

Most rural centres have a Telecentre where you can surf the Net and access your email. Fax and photocopying facilities are also provided.

Special Precautions

Mosquitoes are a nuisance in some areas, and the debilitating Barmah Forest and Ross River viruses are widespread. Take the usual precautions by protecting your skin with repellent and appropriate clothing, and make sure sleeping areas are protected. Other annoying insects include kangaroo ticks, March flies and sand flies (midges).

Stinging jellyfish can be a problem off some beaches (see Swimming p36).

Leaving valuables unsecured in your vehicle is asking for trouble, as it would be anywhere in Australia. Never leave expensive cameras, handbags etc in full view of passers-by, even if you're only away from the car for a few minutes – it will take an accomplished thief just a few seconds to smash their way in. Carry personal documents, medications, prescriptions, credit cards and travel funds with you at all times. Take out travel insurance as well.

Where to Stay

There is plenty of accommodation in the South West, with a hotel, motel or caravan park in most small towns. Tourist areas offer all manner of alternative accommodation such as backpacker hostels, B&Bs and farm stays. The RACWA (see below) publishes annual accommodation and tourist park directories as well as lists of campgrounds in national parks and state forests.

Camping & Caravanning

Public 'bush' campgrounds with basic facilities are found in national parks and state forests and along the coast throughout the South West. Some of these are on shire reserves, hence are the responsibility of local shire offices, while others are managed by CALM – the latter invariably have an excellent standard. Sometimes the two are side-by-side, as at Thomas River in Cape Arid National Park, which can become rather confusing.

Planning the Trip

Planning The Trip

These bush places – particularly shire sites are usually pretty basic. The facilities at most are limited to picnic furniture and long-drop toilets, while others (a rarity) boast hot-water showers and flush toilets. Some are totally informal (i.e. you park wherever you like), or there may be defined bays. A campground may include bays that are suitable for caravans, but there's no such thing as powered sites and there are generally restrictions on the use of generators.

The usual common-sense rules apply:

- Campfires are strictly forbidden during fire danger periods. These vary from shire to shire, but usually as a minimum cover the entire summer – the dates are advertised on roadside signs. Gas fires are prohibited on days of total fire ban.
- All firewood must be brought in.
- Where no bins are provided, take all rubbish with you and dispose of it at an authorised collection point.
- Camp only in existing cleared areas – don't create new ones.
- Don't camp under tree branches that are large enough to cause injury or worse should they come crashing down on your camp.
- If no toilet is provided, bury waste at least 100m from any watercourse.
- Leave your dog at home. Dogs on leashes are permitted in state forests, but being on a leash won't necessarily stop Rover gobbling down a poisoned fox bait.
- Unless otherwise stated, don't use portable generators between 9pm and 8am.
- Limits invariably apply to lengths of stay.
- Don't oblige any wildlife that comes scrounging for a feed. Apart from the fact that foreign foods can be harmful to their health, feeding them encourages aggressive behaviour. It's also against the law.
- Water taken from streams and rainwater tanks should be boiled before drinking.

Beach camping is possible in many areas. While this can be great fun, the risk of getting sandblasted and having your tent turned inside out by a strong sea breeze is high – pack plenty of sand pegs and tie-down rope. Camping behind the foredune might be more enjoyable.

Hema's *Camping Atlas of Western Australia*, by Colin & Prue Kerr, is a state-wide guide, with plenty of useful information relevant to the South West, including excellent maps. *The Guide to Free Camping in the South of WA*, by S & S Collis, is less detailed but describes many more sites.

Camping Fees

The use of established campgrounds in national parks and state forests attracts a fee. Campgrounds with no facilities, or only basic ones, cost $5 per adult per night. Those with toilets, showers and caravan bays (without power) cost $12.50 per site for one or two adults and $5 for extra adults. School-aged children under 16 are generally charged $2.

Getting Around

The South West has a good network of two-lane sealed roads that link Perth and all major centres. You can visit most if not all the region's major attractions and only rarely have to leave the bitumen. Even so, there are plenty of unsealed back roads in the remoter farming and conservation areas. In-depth exploration of state forests and many national parks involves driving on dirt roads and, in some cases, 4WD tracks.

Road conditions in rural areas of the South West are little different to anywhere else in Australia. Roads in farming areas are fenced against wandering stock but kangaroos are always a menace, particularly at dawn and dusk in state forests and the like. Avoid driving at night in these places. Gravel roads tend to have loose surfaces, and single-vehicle accidents caused by excessive speed and/or inexperience are common. Beware of oncoming vehicles, including log trucks, on narrow forestry roads.

You'll find the Royal Automobile Club of Western Australia (RACWA, ☎ 08 9421 4400, www.rac.com.au) at 228 Adelaide Terrace in Perth. Its bookshop sells an excellent range of maps and travel guides, and its bimonthly magazine *Road Patrol* usually contains articles of interest to visiting motorists.

See the Cycling section pp26-27. ■

Bush camping

Chapter Three

What to Do

It has already been said: the South West is tailor-made for outdoor pursuits. You can tackle most of them independently or with commercial operators. The commercial operators who undertake tours on land managed by CALM must be licensed. For a complete list of accredited operators (including the activities that they offer and where these take place), check www.naturebase.net/tourism and follow the links.

The following multi-discipline operators take individual bookings:

- **Adventure In** – abseiling, bushwalking, canoeing, caving and rock climbing in the Margaret River area (✆ 08 9757 2104, www.margs.com.au)
- **Adventure Out Australia** – abseiling, caving, rock climbing and white-water rafting in the outer Perth and Margaret River areas (✆ 08 9472 3919, www.adventureout.com.au)
- **Adventure Pursuits** – abseiling and sand-boarding near Esperance (✆ 0403 009 620)
- **Dekked Out Adventures** – abseiling, bushwalking, kayaking and white-water rafting, mainly in the Bunbury/Margaret River area (✆ 08 9796 1000, dekkedout@iprimus.com.au)
- **Dwellingup Adventures** – bushwalking, canoeing and white-water rafting in the Dwellingup area (✆ 08 9538 1127, www. dwellingupadventures.com.au)
- **Inspiration Outdoors** – bushwalking and canoeing for baby-boomers in the Perth and Margaret River areas (✆ 08 9378 2523, www.inspirationoutdoors.com.au)
- **Merribrook** – abseiling, bushwalking, caving and rock climbing in the Margaret River area (✆ 08 9755 5599, www.merribrook.com.au)
- **Outdoor Discoveries** – abseiling, canoeing, caving, rock climbing (✆ 0407 084 945, www.outdoordiscoveries.com.au)
- **Pemberton Hiking & Canoeing** – bushwalking and canoeing in the Pemberton area (✆ 08 9776 1559, www.pembertonwa.com)
- **Rivergods** – canoeing, kayaking and white-water rafting throughout the South West (✆ 08 9259 0749, www.rivergods.com.au)
- **Shaw Horizons** – abseiling, bushwalking, caving and rock climbing (✆ 08 9343 3363, shawhorizons@myoffice.net.au)
- **Tall Timber Adventure Treks** – bushwalking, camping, canoeing, fishing and mountain biking mainly in the Bridgetown/Pemberton area (✆ 08 9761 7076, www.talltimbertreks.com.au)
- **Wilderness Playgrounds** – abseiling, caving and rock climbing in the Perth Hills and Margaret River areas (✆ 08 9295 3860, www.wildernessplaygrounds.com.au)

Land-Based Activities

Bushwalking

There are literally hundreds of defined bushwalking routes ranging in length from less than 1km to almost 1000km. The region's *pièce de résistance* for long-distance trekkers is the 963km Bibbulmun Track, which links Perth and Albany (see the boxed text). Also outstanding is the 135km Cape-to-Cape Track, between Cape Naturaliste and Cape Leeuwin. In terms of opportunities for sheer enjoyment of nature – not to mention the sense of challenge – these two tracks are among Australia's best.

Overall there's a tremendous diversity in the attractions on offer. Follow a track and you might find yourself admiring wildflowers in a coastal heath, watching birdlife in a pristine wetland, enjoying the view from a mountain top, soaking up the atmosphere of a virgin forest, or walking along a remote beach where the only footprints are your own.

Some tracks are suitable only for fit, well-equipped walkers. Others are fine for families and some have been designed to be wheelchair-friendly. On some routes, such as the Bibbulmun and Cape-to-Cape tracks, you can either walk independently or accompany a CALM-approved guide. Whatever your requirements, you should have little difficulty finding something to suit.

The most comfortable times to go bushwalking are late-winter/early spring (August-October) and early autumn (March-April). Winter is often cold and wet, while hot summer days are best spent keeping cool down at the beach. In warm weather drink plenty of water (not soft drinks or other diuretics like coffee, tea or alcohol), wear a broad-brimmed hat and loose-fitting, light-coloured clothing, and use a good-quality sunscreen on exposed skin.

Be aware that weather conditions can change dramatically and unexpectedly in the Porongurup and Stirling ranges. A warm, sunny day can quickly degenerate into driving rain and cold wind, making hypothermia a real danger if you don't have appropriate clothing with you. Heathlands may be famous for their wildflowers, but the actual plants tend to be very prickly – wear long pants to protect your legs.

If going on long walks, let someone responsible know of your intentions. Also contact them after you've finished your walk, otherwise a search may be initiated.

Information

There is at least rudimentary information available for most public walks, and you can usually pick up leaflets at tourist centres and CALM offices. A swag of routes are described in the three books, *Family Walks in Perth Outdoors*, *More Family Walks in Perth Outdoors* and *Bush Walks in the South-West*, all published by CALM.

Lonely Planet's *Walking in Australia* covers several of the South West's best walks including: the northern end of the Cape-to-Cape Track; the Bluff Knoll and Toolbrunup Peak tracks in Stirling Range National Park; and the Walpole to Peaceful Bay section of the Bibbulmun Track.

CALM's Tracks & Trails Unit (℗ 08 9334 0265) is at 17 Dick Perry Avenue in Kensington, Perth. They don't claim to know everything, but they can direct you to people who do.

Organised Tours

The following operators offer guided walks, mostly on the Bibbulmun and Cape-to-Cape tracks: Adventure In; Dekked Out Adventures; Inspiration Outdoors; Merribrook; Pemberton Hiking Company; Shaw Horizons; Tall Timber Adventure Treks; and Wilderness Playgrounds. See p23 for contact details.

ROB BOEGHEIM

Sunrise at Bluff Knoll

What to Do

Walking the Bibbulmun Track

Stretching 963km between Kalamunda (near Perth) and Albany (on the south coast), the Bibbulmun Track ranks among Australia's finest long-distance walking routes.

For virtually its entire length the track passes through a chain of conservation zones ranging from state forest to national park. Its many highlights include great views and some of the South West's most outstanding natural attractions. You'll also get to know the jarrah, marri, wandoo, karri and tingle. In spring you'll revel in the stunning beauty of the coastal heathlands in full bloom.

The Bibbulmun Track is suitable for walkers of all ages and levels of experience. Most people with reasonable fitness should be able to complete an end-to-end walk in less than eight weeks. Not everyone is interested in a marathon trek, however. Of the thousands of walkers who use the Bibbulmun Track each year, most are only on it for a day or two – or less. There are numerous designated vehicle access points along the way and these make it easy to get on and off the track as you please.

Facilities en route are excellent, with free purpose-built campsites – each with a three-sided timber sleeping shelter, rainwater tank, picnic facilities, cleared tent sites and pit toilet – spaced no more than a day's walk apart. Along the way you pass through, or close to, a string of towns: Dwellingup, Collie, Balingup, Donnelly River Village, Pemberton, Northcliffe, Denmark, Walpole and Peaceful Bay.

The track is marked with yellow triangles showing a *Waugal*. Waugals are important Nyoongar snake ancestors who, among other things, created the river systems here.

For ease of navigation the route has been divided into eight sections, each with its own large-scale map:

Map 1: Kalamunda to North Bannister (Albany Hwy) (138km) – Highlights include the Mundaring Weir and sweeping views from Mt Cuthbert and Mt Vincent.

Map 2: North Bannister to Harvey-Quindanning Rd (125km) – The Dwellingup Forest Centre, the beautiful banks of the Murray River and the spectacular view from Mt Wells are major features.

Map 3: Harvey-Quindanning Rd to Mumballup (93km) – Check the Mumballup Tavern, the historic Long Gully Bridge and the old-growth jarrah forest around Yourdaming Campsite.

Map 4: Mumballup to Brockman Hwy (91km) – Standouts include Balingup township (including the Golden Valley Tree Park), the view down the Blackwood River valley from Cardiac Hill, and Karri Gully.

Map 5: Brockman Hwy to Middleton Rd (168km) – Highlights on this section include Donnelly River Village, One Tree Bridge, Beedelup Falls and Gloucester Tree.

Map 6: Middleton Rd to Broke Inlet Rd (91km) – Beautiful Lake Maringup and the Gardner River are major features.

Map 7: Broke Inlet Rd to William Bay Rd (156km) – Outstanding features include Mandalay Beach, the Tree Top Walk and the view from Conspicuous Cliffs.

Map 8: William Bay Rd to Albany (101km) – The wind farm, coastal heath (in spring) and stunning coastal views make a suitable grand finale for those who have walked all the way from Perth.

There are all sorts of options when it comes to 'doing' the track. While hardened purists have their own criteria for a good time, others may prefer day walks between B&Bs that will do pick-ups and drop offs. Or you may wish to join an organised tour with a CALM-approved guide.

Advice on these and all other matters pertaining to the track is available from the Bibbulmun Track Foundation (✆ 08 9481 0551 or 9321 0649, www.bibbulmuntrack.org.au) at 862 Hay St in Perth – it's above the Mountain Design shop.

Organised Tours

The Bibbulmun Track Foundation organises minimum two-day, two-night walking and accommodation packages based around the towns along the track. Give them your requirements and they'll provide a quote.

Cycling

Cycling is growing in popularity, with many innovative developments such as rail trails (generally shared walk/cycle trails on disused railway alignments), urban pathways and the long-distance Munda Biddi Trail (see the boxed text). By and large the gradients are pretty easy once you get away from the Darling Range, and it's not difficult to find alternatives to busy highways.

The air in WA is dry. (Motor)cyclists should keep up their fluid intake or they could end up like this.

In the metropolitan area there are several good scenic routes mainly on shared pathways. These include the Ride Around the Rivers, which takes you on a 100km circuit of the Swan and Canning rivers; and the Ride Along the Sunset Coast, a 50km coastal ride between Woodman Point and Burns Beach. The network of shared pathways in Kings Park offers a bush cycling experience near the city centre, while the bicycle is king out on Rottnest Island (see pp48-49).

There are a number of cycle paths in the Darling Range near Perth. The booklet *Ride Through the Hills* (Bikewest) describes three scenic loop routes centred on Midland, Kalamunda and Armadale. Each includes numerous points of interest such as wineries, picnic spots, lookouts and historic sites. When completed, the Kep Track will link Mundaring Weir and Northam, while the 70km Railway Reserve Heritage Trail runs from Midland in the west to Wooroloo in the east – a loop includes John Forrest National Park. Last but by no means least, the Munda Biddi Trail heads south along the Darling Scarp from its northern terminus in Mundaring.

Those who don't fancy cycling on busy main roads will find great potential for touring on forestry roads and old logging tracks throughout the South West. However, corrugations can be troublesome and, on the narrower roads, you have to watch out for oncoming traffic. Help slow the spread of dieback by staying out of forest quarantine areas – these are well signposted.

There are several good trails around Margaret River, which is connected by cycle paths to Prevelly (a surfing centre) and Cowaramup. Further south, Northcliffe has mountain bike trails in the surrounding forests, while the mainly one-way Great Forest Trees Drive, which forms an unsealed 48km loop in Shannon National Park, is well worth exploring by bike.

Information & Maps

Probably the best place in Perth for information on cycling in country areas is CALM's Tracks & Trails Unit (☎ 08 9334 0265) at 17 Dick Perry Avenue in Kensington. Bikewest (☎ 08 9216 8000, www.dpi.wa.gov.aus/cycling/) at 441 Murray St in the city is another good source. The Bicycle Transportation Alliance (☎ 08 9420 7210) at 2 Delhi St, West Perth can provide sound practical advice on touring.

Bikewest has a sadly out-of-date but still useful pack of leaflets and maps that describe 29 routes of up to three days between Perth and Walpole.

If heading south, the 1:400,000 *Cycling Down South* map (Bikewest) covers the area from Bunbury to Walpole. It highlights sealed roads that carry relatively little traffic, and describes five mountain bike trails in the vicinity of Balingup, Manjimup, Margaret River and Wellington Dam. See p20 for more on maps.

Bike Hire

The following places have good-quality bicycles for rent:
- **About Bike Hire** – Perth (☎ 08 9221 2665)
- **Down South Camping** – Margaret River (☎ 08 9758 8966)
- **Dwellingup Adventures** – Dwellingup (☎ 08 9538 1127)

Bike Transport

Sadly, Westrail – the South West's major provider of public transport services – isn't very helpful when it comes to carrying bikes on its trains and coaches. South West Coachlines (☎ 08 9324 2333) does the coastal run between Perth and Augusta and is happy to carry bikes.

Events

Every year the Cycle Touring Club of Western Australia (www.clawa.asn.au) holds the On Your Bike, nine-day tour through country WA in springtime, and the 15-day Albany-Perth Tour in April/May.

Organised Tours

West Coast Trail Bike Safaris (✆ 0419 858 209, www.westcoastsafaris.com.au) offers one to three-day tours in the forests between Bunbury and Pemberton. Dirty Detours (✆ 0417 998 816, www.dirtydetours.com) operates in the Margaret River area.

Bird-Watching

The best times to observe the South West's birdlife tend to be early morning and late afternoon, especially in spring and early summer. Arm yourself with medium to high-power binoculars or a telescope, plus a good field guide, and you should get in some memorable bird-watching.

There are numerous birding hot spots in and around Perth. Kings Park and Bold Park are great for honeyeaters including the endemic and the endemic subspecies of the **little wattlebird** (*Anthochaera lunulate*). The urban wetlands are good places to see a variety of water birds; large numbers of migratory waders visit Rottnest Island's lakes and the Swan Estuary Marine Park.

Most birders want to see endemic species, of which there are 11 (see Birds pp16-17), and the good news is that most of them are found quite close to the city. Two prime spots are Wungong Gorge and nearby Bungendore Park, both in the Darling Range Regional Park near Bedfordale. On a good day here you might see the two endemic black-cockatoos as well as western rosellas, red-capped parrots, red-eared firetails, red-winged fairy wrens, western spinebills, western thornbills and white-breasted robins.

Munda Biddi Trail

Designed for mountain bikes, the Munda Biddi Trail will stretch nearly 900km from Mundaring in the Perth Hills to Albany when completed. The first stage of 300km from Mundaring to Collie via Dwellingup is open for business and has quickly become a 'must do' for local and visiting enthusiasts. Indications are that the second stage to Pemberton will be in use by mid-2005.

Munda Biddi means 'path through the forest' in the Nyoongar language, and that sums it up nicely. Like the Bibbulmun Track, it will largely run within the confines of the South Western forests, with jarrah dominating the northern parts and karri in the south.

The gravel-surfaced trail has been designed to cater as much as possible for all ages and levels of experience. It mainly follows forestry tracks and disused railway alignments; gradients are generally easy except in steeper areas like the Darling Range and the slopes of river valleys. Along the way are loops that cater for hard-core cyclists – in Stage One the 45km Waterous Loop provides a connection with Lane Poole Reserve, Waroona Dam and Logue Brook Dam.

There are numerous vehicle access points, and a detailed, large-scale topographic map covers each section. If you don't want to cycle the whole way it's easy to design a tour to suit your own requirements.

The trail is marked throughout with blue triangles that carry a yellow Nyoongar motif. Purpose-built campgrounds are located a comfortable day's ride apart – each consists of a sleeping shelter (capacity 20-25 persons), tent sites, composting toilet, rainwater tanks and picnic facilities. Hot showers will have to wait until you reach the next town, which shouldn't be more than a day away.

For safety's sake cyclists should wear a helmet (a legal requirement in WA) and brightly coloured clothing, and carry a first-aid kit and plenty of drinking water.

For an update on progress and a wealth of general information, go to the Munda Biddi Trail Foundation's website (www.mundabiddi.org.au) or call them on ✆ 0422 112 229. Otherwise contact CALM's Tracks & Trails Unit.

The Denmark-Walpole area is particularly good for bird-watching thanks to its mosaic of major habitats – tall forests, banksia and peppermint woodlands, heathlands, inlet shallows, beaches and farmland. Over 160 species have been recorded here including eight endemics.

A more famous birding location is Two Peoples Bay, to the east of Albany. Sneak around early in the morning and you might be lucky enough to hear if not see the noisy scrub-bird and the western bristle-bird, both endangered endemic species. Also occurring in this general area are two endangered endemic subspecies: the **western ground parrot** *(Pezoporus wallicus flaviventris)*, which occurs at nearby Waychinicup National Park, and the **western whipbird** *(Psophodes nigrogularis nigrogularis)*, which is found at both Waychinicup and Two Peoples Bay. Most of the South West's other endemic species and subspecies can be seen at Two Peoples Bay.

The threatened **mallee fowl** *(Leipoa ocellata)* is widespread in suitable habitat across Australia, but its numbers continue to decline for the usual reasons. Good spots to see these elusive mound-builders include Four-Mile Campsite in Fitzgerald River National Park and Barrets Farm (℡ 08 9835 5026, pmbarret @wn.com.au) near Jerramungup.

Information

Birds Australia's WA office (℡ 08 9383 7749, www.birdswa.iinet.net.au) is at 71 Oceanic Drive in Floreat, a Perth suburb. It publishes a useful booklet on birding sites near Perth as well as a number of regional bird guides and lists that you can download off the web.

There are plenty of websites dealing with birding in the South West. Birds Australia's interesting site gives details of coming activities. Another useful bird site is www.ausbird.com/wa.html – its links include local birder Frank O'Connor's comprehensive coverage of WA's premier birding spots.

Organised Tours

The Stirling Range Retreat adjoining Stirling Range National Park has bird tours – see p90.

Frank O'Connor (℡ 08 9386 5694, www .birdingwa.iinet.net.au) does tailor-made birding tours from Perth.

Based in Busselton, Capricorn Wildlife Tours (℡ 08 9751 3000, tracks@bigpond.com)

does half-day/day bird-watching tours costing $66/88, and longer accommodated tours by arrangement.

Watching Land Mammals

If you sneak around very quietly in the bush at night with a good torch you'll probably spot one or two of the South West's native mammals. The best way to do this is to hold your torch in front of you at about eye level and look along the beam as you move it over the ground or vegetation. When you see an eye-shine (the torchlight reflecting off an animal's eyes), hold the light steady until your eyes have adjusted and you can identify the animal and what it is doing.

CALM's pocket guide *Mammals of the South-West* is a good aid to identifying local mammals and the sorts of environments you can expect to find them in.

Depending on what habitat you're investigating it's quite common to see such animals as kangaroos, wallabies, brush-tailed possums and quendas. However, the chances of spotting one of the region's rarities aren't all that good. The only sure way to see them in the wild is to join a specialised evening tour with a skilled naturalist. These are available at:

- **Barna Mia Sanctuary** – ℡ 08 9881 9200, in the Dryandra Woodland near Narrogin
- **Karakamia Sanctuary** – ℡ 08 9572 3169, in the Perth Hills near Mundaring
- **Perup Forest Ecology Centre** – ℡ 08 9771 7988, near Manjimup

These places are covered in more detail in the regional chapters.

Watching Wildflowers

While some promotional material gives the impression that every spring brings vast, wildly colourful carpets of floral gems, it ain't necessarily so. Still, even in a crook season it's unlikely that Mother Nature's offerings will be disappointing.

The main wildflower period is September/October, with November also being good in the south in places like Stirling Range National Park. Otherwise you'll find a variety of plants in flower no matter what the month. In some places, such as Fitzgerald River National Park, even summer brings outstanding rewards, although of course the experience doesn't compare with spring.

You don't have to go very far from Perth to see stunning displays of wildflowers. At Kings Park and Bold Park, both of which have large areas of native bushland, you can view numerous species without leaving the metropolitan area. A little further afield, the jarrah forests of the Darling Range east of the city are home to many varieties.

Probably the best places to see wildflowers near Perth are the coastal heaths up towards Yanchep, Lancelin and Moore River National Park. The displays in road and conservation reserves in this area are magnificent and make a good day trip from Perth (see Scenic Drives p30). Take plenty of film and be prepared to stop often – wildflowers are hard to appreciate when you're whizzing past them at 110km/h.

There are many, many other places in which to see the South West's wildflowers and it would take a book to describe them all. However, the highlight of all the options would have to be a visit to either the Stirling Range or Fitzgerald River national parks near Albany. Both are world renowned for the diversity of their flora.

Finally, a word of warning. While it's perfectly acceptable to wander through the bush admiring the wildflowers, it is illegal to pick them without a licence, and transgressors may face an on-the-spot fine.

See pp10-14 for more on wildflowers.

Information
The Wildflower Society of WA (℡ 08 9383 7979, www.ozemail.com.au/~wildflowers/) is at 71 Oceanic Drive in Floreat, a Perth suburb – the office opens from 10am to 2.30pm on Tuesdays and Thursdays. Its excellent website is full of useful information, including recommended reference books, events, tours and places to visit.

CALM publishes several pocket references to regional wildflowers. These cost $6.50 each and are available at CALM information centres and tourist offices. WATC's free publication *Western Australian Wildflower Holiday Guide* details several self-drive tours you can do in the South West and elsewhere.

Events
The **Kings Park Wildflower Festival** and the Wildflower Society's **Spring Fling** occur in September, while a number of country towns hold springtime wildflower displays. See the society's website for details.

Organised Tours
West Coast Rail & Coach (℡ 1800 249 522) offers five-day accommodated wildflower tours in the South West costing from $999 twin-share. A naturalist accompanies all tours.

Western Geographic Ecotours (℡ 08 9336 4992, www.westerngeographic.com.au) takes small groups on two-day 4WD wildflower tours. The cost is $325 all-inclusive.

The Stirling Range Retreat offers worthwhile guided wildflower tours. For more details see p90.

Based in Busselton, Capricorn Wildlife Tours (℡ 08 9751 3000, tracks@bigpond.com) does half-day/day wildflower tours costing $66/88, and longer accommodated tours by arrangement.

The Pemberton Hiking Company also does wildflower tours (see the listing at the start of this chapter).

Driving
The South West offers driving to suit all tastes. Some areas, particularly the Wheatbelt, can get a bit monotonous with a gently undulating landscape of farm paddocks that seems neverending. On the other hand, the Southern Forests are often so picturesque that you'll want to stop every 10 minutes to take a photo.

Some of the more interesting drives (e.g. through national parks) may involve some gravel, though this is usually not a problem in a standard car driven with care. Take it easy, not just because of the loose surface but also to spare your tyres. Beware of oncoming traffic on narrow forestry roads. Avoid driving through the dust clouds thrown up by other vehicles – if you can't see, turn your headlights on and pull off the road until the dust has settled.

There's also good four-wheel driving – see below.

Scenic Drives
There are many excellent scenic drives offering a variety of attractions. Hema's *South West Western Australia* touring map shows a number of routes that correspond with locally signposted tourist drives. However, personal favourites include the following (distances are indicative only):

- **Northern Wildflowers.** This 320km loop on the Swan Coastal Plain north of Perth is a real treat when the heath is in full bloom.

Roadside warning near Bunbury

Rather effective radar warning near Beedelup Falls

Depart Perth via Wanneroo Rd, stopping at Yanchep National Park before continuing on to Lancelin for lunch. In the afternoon head east on dirt roads to the Brand Hwy, stopping at Moore River National Park enroute. Return to Perth on the Brand Hwy with a short detour (if time) to Walyunga National Park.

• **Cape Arid Tracks.** This 190km, 4WD (!) route in Cape Arid National Park starts at the Thomas River Campground. From here you drive north to Fisheries Rd, east to Israelite Bay, northwest to Mt Ragged, then southwest back to Fisheries Rd. Much of it is slow going, with many rocky or soft sandy sections, but conditions are generally straightforward. Sections may become impassable after heavy rain. Highlights include the old Israelite Bay telegraph station, the view from Mt Ragged and the sense of space. It's most interesting in spring when the heath is flowering.

• **Tall Timber.** One of the South West's many enjoyable forest drives takes you on mainly sealed back roads between the timber towns of Manjimup and Nannup. Starting at the Manjimup end you head west to One Tree Bridge, then north through karri forest along the Donnelly River to the old Donnelly River Mill (now a holiday village). From here head north to the Brockman Hwy, in jarrah/marri country, where you turn west to Nannup. Watch out for log trucks on this route.

• **Stirling Range.** This short (60km), mainly unsealed drive through Stirling Range National Park links Red Gum Pass Rd in the park's west to Bluff Knoll in the east. Highlights include the diverse flora and dramatic views, particularly of Talyuberlup Peak, Toolbrunup Peak and Bluff Knoll. Beware of loose corners on this road.

• **Cape-to-Cape.** For variety it's hard to beat Caves Rd, the 100km coastal route between Dunsborough and Augusta. All the way along this winding, fully sealed drive there are detours to attractions such as show caves, a karri forest, many great wineries and several famous surfing spots. To see it all, allow at least two days.

• **Nannup-Balingup Rd.** This meandering, 41km drive along the scenic Blackwood River Valley is a 'must do'. The road takes you through steep hills covered in a patchwork of native forest, plantations and farmland, with access to the river at Revelly Bridge and Wrights Bridge.

Four-Wheel Driving

The South West has plenty of options for four-wheel driving, particularly along the southern coast. D'Entrecasteaux, West Cape Howe, Fitzgerald River, Stokes, Cape Le Grand and Cape Arid national parks are popular destinations for 4WD enthusiasts; most of these places offer significant beach drives as well as overland routes to fishing and camping spots. However, there is little opportunity for 4WD touring as such, as the distances involved are generally short. The main touring options are found within Cape Arid National Park and state forest areas. Another is the coastal track between Lancelin and Cervantes.

Vehicles lacking low-range gearing and/or good ground clearance are unlikely to get through the sections of deep, soft sand found on most coastal tracks, particularly in summer. Anyone attempting such tracks should have a tyre gauge and pump (or air-compressor) on board, as tyre deflation is usually essential. Ignore this advice if you're one of those odd people who enjoy spending their days off digging themselves out of bogs. Another reason to deflate your tyres is to keep the track from being chopped up.

The roads within Cape Arid NP contain frequent bog holes and may be impassable when wet

As a rule of thumb, drop light truck tyres to 18 psi and engage 4WD before entering soft sandy sections. If you're running fats or soft-walled tyres, check with the manufacturer for recommended minimum pressures. Hitting the sand in third-gear low-range and with plenty of throttle (but not too much) usually allows you to power through without damaging either the track or your vehicle. It's important to maintain momentum, so try to avoid changing gear halfway through – use established wheel ruts, as the sand there will have been compacted.

There's always the chance of a head-on collision on narrow 4WD tracks. Keep the speed down wherever your view in front is restricted, and send someone ahead at dune crossings

Tyre deflation is usually essential in soft sandy sections, even if reinflation afterwards can be a tedious process. Cheap compressors (as shown here) can take ages and are known to burn out, so make sure you have a backup

to warn of oncoming vehicles. A bright-orange pennant secured to a pole tied to your bull bar will warn others of your approach.

When beach driving it's generally a requirement of the managing authority that you stay below the high-water mark. Apart from anything else, this will stop you running over the nests of the endangered hooded plover, which lays its eggs in sand scapes between the high-water mark and the base of the sand hills. Always check tide times before embarking on long beach drives, and don't attempt to cross river mouths unless you know that it's safe to do so.

Useful websites for planning purposes include www.exploroz.com (track notes etc) and www.trackcare.com.au (news, events and links). Finally, it's common sense to seek local advice before committing yourself to the unknown – you might just receive that invaluable mud map or useful tip.

Organised Tours

A good option for novice four-wheel drivers is to join a tag-along tour. Such tours enable you to visit remote areas in your own vehicle, secure in the knowledge that expert advice and assistance are at hand when things go wrong. Tour operators providing this service include:

* **Esperance Eco-Discovery Tours** –
  ✆ 0407 737 261,
  www.esperancetours. com.au
* **Rod's 4WD Tag-along Tours** – Busselton
  (✆ 0417 929 750)

Horse Riding

A number of places offer horse rides, and the following have some interesting options for competent riders. For obvious reasons, the longer treks aren't available in hot weather:

Horse riding at Esperance Bay

Abseiling requires steady nerves, but it's easier than climbing and you won't forget the experience

- **Langford Hill Riding Farm** – Waroona, south of Pinjarra (✆ 08 9733 1455)
- **Lazy R Pony Stud** – Denmark (✆ 08 9840 9281)
- **Pioneer Trails of WA** – near Pinjarra (✆ 08 9581 1384, trails@southwest.com.au)
- **The Stables Yanchep** – Yanchep, north of Perth (✆ 08 9561 1606, www.stablesyanchep.com.au)
- **Xanadu Horse Rides** – Esperance (✆ 08 9075 9029, 0429 920 957)

Abseiling & Rock Climbing

You'll find some great spots for abseiling and climbing, and there are several popular sites in the granite quarries of the Perth Hills. However, the best ones are all down south. The closest of these to Perth is Leeuwin-Naturaliste National Park, where the granite sea cliffs of Wilyabrup are the main draws. There are limestone cliffs in this area too, not to mention several caves where you can combine abseiling with adventure caving.

Further south, between Denmark and Albany, the towering dolerite sea cliffs in West Cape Howe National Park offer some of the state's most exciting climbing. Closer to Albany are the Amphitheatre (near The Gap) and Peak Head, both in Torndirrup National Park. Peak Head is a huge granite dome that drops sheer for 120m into the ocean – getting there involves an enjoyable 2.5km walk from the Stony Hill car park. Climbing routes near The Gap – a major scenic attraction – are short, but easier to get to.

The South West's major climbing challenge is the 300m-high north face of Bluff Knoll, the highest point in Stirling Range National Park. Most of the climbs on this magnificent feature take at least six hours to complete, and none is suitable for novices. Elsewhere in the park there are some excellent climbing routes on the imposing Talyuberlup Peak.

Other places worth visiting include Porongurup National Park (Gibraltar Rock, Marmabup Rock and Castle Rock) and Mt Frankland National Park. All these venues are granite domes with good accessibility and great views.

Information & Permits

A permit must be obtained from CALM before abseiling in national parks and nature reserves. You don't need a permit to go rock climbing, but you must register your intentions with the rangers – some areas, such as The Gap near

ROB VAN DRIESUM

Rock climbing at West Cape Howe

Albany, are off limits to climbers. It's a requirement that climbs be carried out in accordance with the code of ethics established by the Climbers Association of Western Australia (CAWA, www.climberswa.asn.au).

Perth climb shops such as Mainpeak, with outlets in Cottesloe (☏ 08 9385 2552) and Subiaco (☏ 08 9388 9072), and The Hangout (☏ 08 9371 9939) are good sources of information. CAWA's site includes details on climbing areas and new routes.

Shane Richardson's *West Australian Rock* (Climb West, 2002) is a general guide to the state's best rock climbing venues. Climb West's website www.climbwest.com.au has plenty of useful information.

Organised Tours

The following operators offer rock-climbing and/or abseiling courses and tours: Adventure In; Adventure Out Australia; Dekked Out Adventures; Merribrook; Outdoor Discoveries; Shaw Horizons; and Wilderness Playgrounds. See p23 for contact details.

Adventure Caving

The best opportunities for adventure caving are found in Leeuwin-Naturaliste National Park. Around 190 limestone caves have been discovered here but only a tiny percentage is open to the general public (see p64 for the ones you can visit.)

For the good oil on adventure caving in Leeuwin-Naturaliste National Park, contact the staff at Calgardup Cave (☏ 08 9757 7422) and visit the Western Australian Speleological Group's website (http://wasg.iinet.net.au).

Those who'd like to go caving away from the mob, should consider a self-guided exploration of Calgardup and Giants caves, both on Caves Rd. These are fun for novices and advanced cavers alike, and there is experienced staff on site to answer your questions. Helmets and lights are supplied as part of the entrance fee.

Open daily, **Calgardup Cave** has boardwalks throughout and is suitable for all ages. Its features include an underground stream and lake, and some pretty limestone formations. Allow 40 minutes for a good look.

Giants Cave, also known as Mammoth Cave, is quite a bit larger and takes around an hour to explore. It features huge chambers and, at 83m, is one of the region's deepest caves. Some scrambling and ladder climbing is required, so wear appropriate clothing and sturdy footwear. The cave only opens over school holiday periods and long weekends.

Another 14 caves may be visited in the company of a CALM-approved guide. They provide a variety of experiences and cover all grades of difficulty, so you should be able to find something to suit your requirements. Four of these caves can only be accessed by abseiling. One of the most popular is **Bride's Cave**, where the entrance is a collapsed doline about 30m across and 30m deep. You can also abseil into Calgardup and Giants caves.

Entry to all other caves is restricted to members of the Australian Speleological Federation in the company of a recognised speleological club. The local organisation is Cavers Leeuwin Inc (☏ 08 9758 7079).

Ask at Calgardup for an up-to-date list of CALM's accredited cave-tour operators.

What to Do

Water-Based Activities

Fishing

Fishing is a hugely popular pastime in the South West. So much so, in fact, that concerns over the long-term future of this activity have brought many restrictions in recent years. You'll often hear how it's necessary to get well out to sea these days to do any good, which is as good an indication of stock depletion as any.

There is no shortage of boat charter operators ready to take you out to where the action is. For bottom-fishers the prize is the dhufish, a powerful fighter and delicious table species that can reach 30kg. Don't confuse dhufish with eastern staters' jewfish, which is just another name for mulloway. Other common deep-water (i.e. 40-50m) catches include pink snapper, Samsonfish, blue groper, blue morwong and harlequin.

Back on shore, hundreds of km of beautiful beaches are littered with holes and gutters that beg you to cast a line into them. Many prime locations can only be reached in 4WD vehicles, or by walking for a km or two, or three.

One standout event on local fishing calendars is the arrival of vast schools of Australian salmon on their annual spawning run along the south coast into the Indian Ocean. The fish begin their migration in early February and reach Perth in April/May, creating a flurry of activity from beach anglers – names like Salmon Holes, Salmon Bay and Salmon Beach indicate some of the hot spots. Australian Salmon is by no means a great eating fish, but it does put up a tremendous struggle when hooked (what wouldn't?). Other common species caught off ocean beaches include herring ("ruff" or "tommy ruff" to eastern staters), tailor, mulloway, shark, skippy (trevally), tarwhine (silver bream) and yellowtail and sand whiting.

You can also do well off the innumerable rock ledges and platforms that dot the coastline. However, you have to be extremely careful where these places are exposed to ocean swells, which means most of the coast between Dunsborough and Esperance. Anglers are drowned every year after being swept from their rocky perches by enormous surges of water called king waves. It's a good idea to wear a life jacket, wetsuit and head protection (surfing helmets are ideal) when fishing in such places, and if anchor points have been provided, use them.

Rock fishers should seek local advice before venturing onto any area that could be suspect. Remember that some of the most dangerous places appear perfectly safe until the next big wave comes along.

The larger estuaries can yield a fine array of species, with black bream being among the most popular – they're a challenge to catch, put

Australian Salmon is not a great fish to eat but it's a great fish to catch

Beware of king waves when fishing from coastal rocks

up a good fight and are an excellent table fish. Other common catches include King George whiting, flathead, flounder and cobbler (catfish). Juvenile snapper are a feature of some estuaries, such as the Wilson Inlet near Denmark. Blue manna crabs (see the boxed text p 44) are one of the big attractions of estuarine waters.

Many dams and rivers have been stocked with brown and rainbow trout, but not all are accessible to the public – CALM, the Water & Rivers Corporation, shires and private land-holders have blocked off numerous places.

A licence – available from Australia Post outlets – is required for all freshwater angling, as well as for abalone, rock lobster, marron and net fishing. Bag limits apply to trout, cobbler and marron (a large yabby), but there is no limit on redfin perch.

Some trout waters are open all year, while others are closed from the beginning of May to the end of July.

Information

The Department of Fisheries (✆ 08 9482 7333, www.fish.wa.gov.au) publishes leaflets on minimum legal size limits, bag sizes and seasonal closures. These are widely available from CALM information centres, tourist offices, post offices and tackle shops. Check the website for information about accessible trout fisheries.

There are no fishing guidebooks specific to the South West, but the following state-wide references are worth getting hold of:

- *Fishing the Wild West*, by Ross Cusack and Mike Roennfeldt (West Australian Newspapers, 2002), is a handy glove-box sized reference that describes a number of sought-after species and how and where to catch them.
- *Kurt Blanksby & Frank Porker's Fishing Guide to Western Australia* (Australian Fishing Network, 2003) is too big for the glove box, but makes a good reference during the planning phase. Its maps are excellent and there are plenty of interesting fish facts.

Also check Friday's edition of *The West Australian* newspaper, which has several pages devoted to fishing.

Channel Nine's website www.fishingwa .com has plenty of useful information including fact sheets, species, fishing tips and wheelchair-accessible fishing spots.

Finally, speciality tackle shops are invariably founts of knowledge on all aspects of the local scene.

Boat Charters

You'll find charter-fishing operators in most major coastal centres from Perth's northern suburbs around to Esperance. The following take individual bookings, and you can expect to pay from $130 all-inclusive for a day on the water:

Perth Area
- **Anchor Boat Charters** – ✆ 08 9306 1022, www.anchorcharters.com.au
- **Apache Charters** – ✆ 0417 968 372, www.apachecharters.com.au
- **Blue Juice Charters** – ✆ 0402 040 312, www.bluejuicecharters.com.au
- **Blue Lightning Charters** – ✆ 0408 956 776, mills@multiline.com.au
- **Boatwest Charters & Cruises** – ✆ 08 9430 9691, www.boatwest.com.au
- **Hillary's Fishing Charters** – ✆ 08 9447 6014, www.fishingcharter.com.au
- **Indian Ocean Fishing Safaris** – ✆ 0417 180 715
- **Mills Charters** – ✆ 08 9246 5334, www.millscharters.com.au
- **Leeuwin Marine Group** – ✆ 08 9331 5030, leeuwinmarinegroup@hotmail.com
- **Nelson Boat Charters** – ✆ 08 9305 1521
- **Offshore Fishing Charters** – ✆ 08 9417 2316
- **Rock Island Charters** – ✆ 0428 929 643, www.deepwatercharters.com.au
- **Sea Spray Leisure & Fishing Charters** – ✆ 0409 295 918, kylie@seaspraycharters.com.au
- **Shikari Charters** – ✆ 08 9528 1602
- **True Blue Charters** – ✆ 08 9331 4054, truebluecharters@bigpond.com.au
- **Warrior Princess Charters** – ✆ 1300 555 167, www.warriorprincess.com.au

Mandurah
- **Aqualib Marine Charters** – ✆ 08 9586 9778, www.aqualib.com
- **Blue Chip Offshore Charters** – ✆ 08 9582 9887, www.bluechipcharters.com.au

- **Blue Lightning Charters** –
  ✆ 0408 956 776, mills@multiline.com.au
- **Mandurah Fishing Charters** –
  ✆ 0417 952 534,
  richard@mandurahfishing.cjb.net
- **Port Bouvard Charters** – ✆ 08 9534 2582,
  info@portbouvardcharters.com.au
- **Rock Island Charters** – ✆ 0428 929 643,
  www.deepwatercharters.com.au

Dunsborough/Augusta
- **Augusta Eco-Cruises** – ✆ 08 9758 4003,
  seadragon@westnet.com.au
- **Naturaliste Charters** – ✆ 08 9755 2276,
  www.whales-australia.com
- **Seafari Charters** – ✆ 08 9757 1050,
  www.villacrisafina.com/seafari

Albany
- **Blueback Charters** – ✆ 0427 374 420
- **Spinners Charters** – ✆ 08 9841 7151,
  www.spinnerscharters.com.au

Esperance
- **Duke Charters** – ✆ 08 9076 6223
- **Esperance Diving & Fishing** –
  ✆ 08 9071 5111,
  www.esperancedivingandfishing.com.au
- **Scooters Eco Jet Charters** –
  ✆ 08 9072 0271

Swimming

The South West has many magnificent coastal beaches, including a couple of famous ones in Perth. Most of them are perfectly safe for swimming but many are not. The presence of rips and undertows – which usually aren't obvious until you're caught in one – makes some beaches downright dangerous for swimmers and novice surfers. Beaches patrolled by surf life-savers have red-and-yellow flags placed to indicate the safe areas (swim between the flags). Seek local advice wherever there are no flags or warning signs.

Surf Life Saving Western Australia's website at www.mybeach.com.au includes a useful Beach Updates section.

The local species of **box jellyfish** (*Carybdea xaymacana*) is most prevalent in summer and autumn in sheltered bays between Cape Naturaliste and Geraldton. Also called 'stingers', these small creatures are not to be confused with the notorious stingers (or box jellyfish) of the tropics, though their venom-charged tentacles can still deliver a painful sting. While this may be uncomfortable, the victim rarely requires hospitalisation and, as far as we know, no fatalities have ever occurred. The recommended treatment is to apply a hot compress to the affected area for about 10 minutes, then apply ice. This means taking an esky and a large thermos to the beach.

Swimming with Marine Mammals

Interacting with wild bottlenose dolphins is a fascinating experience and you can do it on supervised "dolphin encounter" swims at Bunbury, Mandurah and Rockingham (a suburb south of Perth). Only operators approved by CALM are permitted to undertake such tours, which cost around $140 per person and are usually available from the beginning of September to the end of May. The idea is that you relax in the water and enjoy the dolphins' company – they don't do tricks, and interfering with them in any way (such as trying to touch or feed them) is strictly forbidden.

You might find yourself sharing the water with dolphins and sea lions on diving and snorkelling trips to such places as Carnac Island and the Shoalwater Islands Marine Park, both near Perth. An inquisitive sea lion might swim up to you, in which case remain as still as possible with your hands by your side to

Swimming at Yallingup Beach

Waiting for the dolphins at Koombana Bay, Bunbury

avoid frightening it. If it becomes aggressive or overly playful, slowly move away and leave the water. Never attempt to touch one.

Whale-Watching

Whale-watching is an extremely popular activity from May to December, when humpback and southern right whales can be seen close to shore on their annual breeding and calving migrations. See p15 for more on whales.

While the two species are superficially similar in appearance (they're both big and black) it's reasonably easy to tell them apart. Humpbacks have extremely long, narrow flippers, small dorsal fins and white bellies, while southern rights have broad, triangular flippers and distinctive white lumps on their heads, and lack dorsal fins. Both grow to around 18m in length, but southern rights are much bulkier. On their return journey humpbacks often put on spectacular displays of fin and tail slapping, breaching and rolling. The characteristic arched or 'hump' back that you see as a humpback whale submerges is another aid to identification.

The sperm whale is another species being seen with increasing frequency, particularly in the Albany area. Growing to a maximum length of 18m and weighing up to 60 tonnes, this creature is easily recognisable by its rectangular head.

Humpbacks and southern rights are often spotted from lookout points such as Cape Naturaliste, Cape Leeuwin and Point D'Entrecasteaux as they move along the coast. Indeed, at some places, such as Dolphin Cove in Cape Arid National Park, you can watch the calves being born just metres away. Generally, however, you'll need medium-powered binoculars or a telescope. The best way to observe them is from a boat, and regular whale-watching tours depart from most towns along the coast. The main whale-watching centres are Albany and Augusta.

Groups of bottlenose dolphins are a common sight throughout the year right along the South West coast. These friendly, intelligent animals have become the centre of a whole new industry, which hopefully won't harm them in the long run. As well as interacting with them in the water (see the earlier Swimming with Marine Mammals section), you can observe them on the boat cruises that operate out of many places along the coast. The

Dolphin Discovery Centre in Bunbury (p59) is a 'must see' if you're interested in learning about these fascinating creatures.

Sailing

The South West coast offers ideal sailing conditions between mid-November and mid-April. There are no crowds, no pollution and nothing harmful in the water apart from the odd shark. However, opportunities for self-drive (bare-boat) and skippered charters seem rather thin on the water.

One of the few operators is Fremantle-based Rottnest Yacht Charters (℗ 08 9336 5952, www.rottnestyachtcharters.com). Their boat carries a maximum of six/nine people for overnight/day cruises, and costs $450/790 for one/two days.

Another is South West Yacht Charters (℗ 08 9721 7664, www.swyachtcharters.com.au) in Busselton. You can charter a luxury Jeanneau 37 and cruise the clear waters of Geographe Bay, calling in to secluded beaches and maybe doing a spot of fishing or snorkelling.

For a totally different experience, the tall ship *Leeuwin* (℗ 08 9430 4105, www.leeuwin.com) offers a range of adventure and environmental discovery voyages along the western coast between Esperance and Darwin. All participants are required to be reasonably fit – those over 50 years of age must produce a medical certificate. The *Leeuwin* is based in Fremantle.

Canoeing & Kayaking

The South West has a number of mainly short streams that are suitable for canoeing and kayaking. Most significant in terms of long-distance canoeing is the Blackwood River, which can be paddled for hundreds of km in winter. Trees and the odd grade 1-2 rapid are the main hazards here. In summer the river is canoeable between Nannup and Hardy Inlet, a distance of 147km.

Next is the Avon River, which in late winter/early spring can be canoed all the way from Northam to Perth, a distance of about 160km. The Avon is the venue for a gruelling, 134km-long white-water race called the Avon Descent (see Northam p99). Novices should confine their activities to the Northam-Toodyay section and downstream of Bells Rapids, on the upper Swan.

Most rivers dry up during the summer drought, but it's an entirely different story in winter and early spring. At the height of the season, kayakers with advanced skills will find plenty to excite them on the Avon, Blackwood, Deep, Frankland and Murray rivers. Most have steep gradients and run either completely or partly through forested country, so there is an ever-present danger of becoming wrapped around a tree or caught in a log jam or tea-tree thicket. As a general rule, novices should stay off the water when streams are in flood.

When spring arrives things begin to calm down: the dramatic reduction in stream flows brings an opportunity for less-proficient canoeists to get among the action. The Swan and Canning near Perth and the lower reaches of the Blackwood, Frankland, Moore and Murray rivers are all good venues for a quiet paddle in summer. If you're in a canoe it's best to stay out of the larger estuaries such as the Broke, Nornalup, Peel and Wright inlets. There are protected sections, but the choppy conditions often experienced on these open bodies of water generally make them better suited to kayaks.

There are some good sea-kayaking venues around the coast. Enthusiasts will take one look at the bays and islands around Esperance and Albany and automatically reach for their paddles. These areas feature strong currents, big swells and wind, which makes them unsuited for novices. Less hazardous is the indented coastline north of Dunsborough and the islands in Shoalwater Islands Marine Park, south of Perth.

Information

CALM offices are good places to start asking about the rivers that flow through national parks and state forests. If the rangers don't have first-hand knowledge they'll be able to point you towards someone who does.

Terry Bolland of Canoeing Down Under (© 08 9378 1333, www.canoeingdownunder .com.au), a Perth-based canoe shop, is an acknowledged expert on the local canoeing and kayaking scenes, and is happy to help with what advice he can. Terry runs kayaking courses for those hardy souls intending to tackle the Avon Descent.

Neville Hamilton of Blackwood River Canoeing (© 08 9756 1209, blackwoodriver canoeing@wn.com.au) down near Nannup knows all about the Blackwood's lower reaches.

Otherwise the website http://members .iinet.net.au/~rokhor/canoe has loads of useful information. For river levels, refer to www.wrc.wa.gov.au (the Water & Rivers Commission's site) – only rivers between the Avon and Blackwood inclusive are metered.

The *Canoe & Kayak Guide to Western Australia*, by Martin Chambers (Hesperian Press, 2000), is a handy reference available from CALM information centres, tourist offices and canoe shops. Also useful (if you can get hold of them) are the canoe notes put out by the Department of Sport & Recreation. They're out of date, but still make good references.

Terry Bolland's *Canoeing Down Under* (Terry Bolland, 2001) covers the Avon and Swan rivers from Northam to Perth, with numerous maps and descriptions of the rapids.

Canoe/Kayak Hire

Along with numerous other operators, Blackwood River Canoeing, and Rivergods, both of which have been around a long time, offer kayaking and/or canoeing trips.

Rivergods has a full range of equipment for hire, as do Blackwood River Canoeing, Dekked Out Adventures in Bunbury, and Dwellingup Adventures in Dwellingup. See p23 for contact details.

Diving & Snorkelling

The South West has many excellent dive spots. These include wrecks both large and small, and, thanks to the Leeuwin Current, a huge diversity of marine life including many tropical species. Rottnest Island is the most popular area with divers and snorkellers, partly by virtue of its proximity to Perth and partly because there are over 200 interesting sites to choose from.

Marmion Marine Park and Shoalwater Marine Park, both on the Perth metropolitan coast, feature eroded limestone reefs inhabited by a stunning array of fish and invertebrates. Diving at the Busselton Jetty is akin to swimming in a giant, well-stocked aquarium. Marine life is also a major attraction at Albany and Esperance.

There are several great wrecks, including the 174m-long bulk carrier *Sanko Harvest* – said to be the world's second-largest diveable wreck – which sank near Esperance in 1991 after running onto rocks. The guided-missile destroyer HMAS *Swan* was scuttled off Dunsborough in 1997 to form a dive wreck. More recently another destroyer, HMAS *Perth*, met a similar fate near

Albany. Off Lancelin there's the wreck of the *Key Biscayne*, a huge oil-exploration rig sitting upside down in 40m of water.

CALM publishes two guidebooks, *Dive & Snorkel Sites in Western Australia* and *More Dive & Snorkel Sites in Western Australia*. Between them they describe around 60 locations around the South West coast.

As the following list indicates, there are numerous dive operators:

Perth's Northern Beaches
- **Mindarie Diving Academy** -
  ✆ 08 9305 7113
- **Sorrento Quay Dive Shop**
  ✆ 08 9448 6343,
  www.sorrentoquaydive.com.au

Perth/Fremantle
- **Dive In** – ✆ 08 9314 6466
- **Dive, Ski & Surf** ✆ 08 9336 4355,
  www.diveskisurf.com
- **Dolphin Dive** – ✆ 08 9336 6286,
  www.dolphindiveshop.com
- **Dolphin Scuba Diving** – ✆ 08 9353 2807,
  www.dolphinscuba.com.au
- **Perth Diving Academy** – ✆ 08 9430 4393,
  www.perthdiving.com.au
- **West Australian Dive Centre** –
  ✆ 08 9421 1883, www.watravelanddive.com

Rockingham
- **Bell Scuba** ✆ 08 9527 9028,
  www.bellscuba.com.au
- **Scubanautics** ✆ 08 9527 4447,
  scuba@accessin.com.au

Rottnest Island
- **Rottnest Malibu Dive** – ✆ 08 9292 5111,
  www.rottnestdiving.com.au

Mandurah
- **David Budd Diving Academy** –
  ✆ 08 9535 1520, dbdiving@bigpond.net.au
- **Mandurah Diving Academy** –
  ✆ 08 9581 2566,
  divemda@accessin.com.au
- **Mandurah Dive & Eco Charters** –
  ✆ 08 9537 8804,
  info@mandurahdiveandeco.com.au.
- **Mandurah Marina Dive Centre** –
  ✆ 08 9586 1000,
  mandmarinecomm@bigpond.com

Bunbury
- **Bunbury Dive Charters** – ✆ 08 9721 1785
- **Coastal Water Dive** – ✆ 08 9721 7786

Busselton
- **Busselton Naturaliste Diving Academy**
  – ✆ 08 9752 2096, www.natdive.com
- **The Dive Shed** – ✆ 08 9754 1615,
  www.diveshed.com.au

Dunsborough
- **Cape Dive** – ✆ 08 9756 8778,
  www.capedive.com
- **Bay Dive** – ✆ 08 9756 8577,
  www.baydive.com

Margaret River
- **Seafari Charters** – ✆ 08 9757 1050,
  www.villacrisafina.com/seafari

Albany
- **Albany Dive.Com** – ✆ 08 9842 6886,
  www.albanydive.com
- **Albany Scuba Diving Academy** –
  ✆ 08 9842 3101, albscuba@bigpond.net.au
- **Dive Albany** – ✆ 08 9841 7176,
  www.divealbany.com.au.

Esperance
- **Esperance Diving & Fishing** –
  ✆ 08 9071 5111, www.esperancediving
  andfishing.com.au

Surfing

Surfing is one of those activities that many people would like to master, but for various reasons (e.g. "I'm too old!") never get around to. Well, here's your chance! There are good training waves right around the coast, and accredited surfing schools operate at Albany, Esperance, Lancelin, Margaret River, Secret Harbour (near Mandurah), Trigg (a northern Perth suburb) and Yallingup.

There is no shortage of waves of international repute, either. The coastline between Cape Naturaliste and Cape Leeuwin is famous for its many powerful breaks, several of which are world class. Eastwards from Augusta the coast is noted for its large southerly swells. However, some good spots are hard to get to (e.g. Black Point) and the wind often ruins things. In the right conditions you'll find memorable surfing at places like Ocean Beach (near Denmark), Sand Patch and Middletons Beach (both near Albany), and Wylie Bay (near Esperance). Rottnest Island, off Perth, has a couple of great breaks on the ocean side.

What to Do

Information

For information on anything to do with the local surfing scene, contact Surfing Western Australia (☎ 08 9448 0004, www.surfingaustralia.com) at 360 West Coast Drive, in Trigg.

Matt Terry's *Waxed – A Guide to Surfing Hot Spots in South Western Australia* covers 100 locations including access and the best conditions.

Special Events

The South West hosts numerous surfing

- **Salomon (Margaret River) Masters** – international short-board event at Surfers Point in March/April
- **Sunsmart Women's Classic** – international women's short-board event at Surfers Point in March/April
- **Whalebone Classic** – national long-board event at Cottesloe in July
- **Malibu Classic** – national long-board event at Yallingup in November/December

Surfing Schools

The South West has a number of surfing schools and you'll find them at the following places:

Perth Area
- **Surfing Western Australia** – at Trigg and Scarborough Beach (☎ 08 9448 0004, www.surfingaustralia.com)

Mandurah Secret Harbour
- **Big Wave Surfing School** – ☎ 08 9524 7671, www.bigwavesurfingschool.com.
- **Lets Go Surfing** – ☎ 08 9537 3709
- **Surf Academy** – ☎ 08 9757 3850, joshpal@westnet.com.au

Margaret River Area
- **Surf Academy** – ☎ 08 9757 3850, joshpal@westnet.com.au
- **Yallingup Surf School** – ☎ 08 9755 2755, yallingupsurfschool@westnet.com.au

Denmark
- **South Coast Surfing** – ☎ 08 9840 9041

Albany
- **Wild West Adventures** – ☎ 0418 929 517

Esperance
- **Esperance Surfing Academy** – ☎ 08 9071 1432

Windsurfing & Kitesurfing

The fresh sea breezes that threaten to drive many people insane during the warmer months create perfect conditions for windsurfing and the relatively new sport of kitesurfing. In fact, some of the South West's windsurfing spots are considered among the best in Australia. Lancelin, a little fishing town north of Perth, is on the world circuit – in January the Ocean Classic takes place over three days at Lancelin and Ledge Point, a tiny fishing community 10km south. At Lancelin you get slalom conditions right off the beach, and the waves allow for some huge jumps.

Other good places include Cervantes (windier than Lancelin, but lacks the waves – excellent for kitesurfing, though), Perth (Swan River and coastal beaches are good for begin-

The Leeuwin Current

To dive or snorkel at places like Parker Point (Rottnest Island) and the Busselton jetty is to enter an aquatic wonderland made up of around 400 species of tropical and subtropical fish, invertebrates, corals and sponges. This huge diversity is made possible by the Leeuwin Current, a narrow band of warm tropical water that flows southward from the Sunda Shelf – between northwest Australia and Indonesia – to Cape Leeuwin, then eastwards into the Great Australian Bight before petering out on the west coast of Tasmania.

As well as being warm and clear, the waters of the Leeuwin Current are low in nutrients. These conditions do not favour the production of large quantities of finfish, but are ideal for invertebrates such as crayfish. The current transports the larvae of tropical marine animals and, because it flows most strongly in autumn and winter, its warming influence makes it possible for these animals to survive much further south than would otherwise be the case.

Windsurfing and kitesurfing on the Swan Estuary

Denis O'Byrne

ners and advanced), Margaret River (great waves, but not for beginners), and Augusta (can blow on the estuary for days on end).

The website www.windsurfwa.com contains lots of information for windsurfers and kitesurfers, including sailing spots and gear hire.

Windsurfing Schools

It takes a rank amateur about six hours tuition to learn the basic skills of windsurfing, and this costs around $120. Kitesurfing and/or windsurfing schools operate at the following places:

Lancelin
- **Werner's Hot Spot** – ✆ 08 9655 1553, www.auswind.com.au

Bunbury
- **Margaret River Kitesurfing & Windsurfing** – ✆ 0419 959 053, www.mrkiteandsail.com.au

Perth Area
- **Go Windsurfing – Rockingham** – ✆ 0438 853 785, www.gowindsurfing.com
- **Pelican Point Wind Sports – Swan River** – ✆ 08 9386 1830, www.pelicanwindsurfing.com.au

Margaret River Area
- **Margaret River Kitesurfing & Windsurfing** – ✆ 0419 959 053, www.mrkiteandsail.com.au

White-Water Rafting

Opportunities for white-water rafting are generally restricted to the winter months, when local streams are in full spate. The most popular venues are the Avon and Murray rivers, both with rapids classified as grade three or higher. However, if you want to go rafting in summer, the Collie River is an option as water is released from the dam then to feed irrigation channels.

Adventure Out Australia, Dekked Out Adventures, Dwellingup Adventures and Rivergods all offer white-water rafting trips. See p23 for contact details.

Aerial Activities

Gliding (Soaring)

There are several gliding clubs in the South West and all welcome visiting fliers:
- **Beverley Soaring Society – Beverley** (✆ 0407 385 361, www.beverley-soaring.org.au)
- **Gliding Club of Western Australia – Cunderdin** (✆ 0409 683 159, www.glidingwa.com.au)
- **Narrogin Gliding Club – Narrogin** (✆ 0407 088 314, www.gfa.org.au/narrogin)
- **Stirlings Gliding Club – Cranbrook** (✆ 08 9844 4163)

Hang-Gliding & Paragliding

The South West's premier hang-gliding venues are near Albany. This region includes several great coastal sites such as well-known Shelleys Beach (in West Cape Howe National Park), which is arguably the South West's top hang-gliding spot, and Sand Patch. Summer is the main season for the south coast, and there are sites to suit regardless of wind direction.

Other spots worth seeking out are in Cape Le Grand National Park (near Esperance), Leeuwin-Naturaliste National Park (in the Margaret River area southwest of Perth), the Darling Scarp, and the Avon Valley between Toodyay and York. Generally a permit is required to hang-glide or paraglide in national parks.

The web page of the Hang Gliding Association of Western Australia, www .hgfa.asn.au/~hgawa/, includes a comprehensive site guide and links to local clubs.

Sky Sports (℗ 08 9451 9969, www .hanglide.com.au) and the West Australian Paragliding Academy (℗ 08 9299 6228, www.waparagliding.com) do tours along the south coast.

Hot-Air Ballooning

Based in Northam, about 96km northeast of Perth, Windward Balloon Adventures (℗ 08 9621 2000, www.windwardballooning .com.au) conducts early-morning hot-air balloon flights over the scenic Avon Valley from April to late November. The one-hour flight costs $200 per adult on weekdays ($250 on weekends and public holidays), including champagne and a cooked breakfast.

Parachuting

If you've never tried skydiving, then now is your chance. Options include:

- **Skydive Express – York**
  (℗ 1800 355 833, www.skydive.com.au)
- **Sky Dive Perth – Perth** (℗ 08 9414 1441, www.skydiveperth.com.au)
- **Southern Sky Divers – Busselton**
  (℗ 0439 979 897,
  www.southernskydivers.com.au)
- **WA Skydiving Academy – Perth**
  (℗ 1300 137 855,
  www.waskydiving.com.au)

A tandem jump from 12,000 feet costs around $350, while an accelerated free fall is around $500, including instruction. ∎

Hang-gliding at Shelleys Beach

Chapter Four

Perth & Surrounds

Western Australia's beautiful capital offers many great opportunities for outdoor pursuits, with some magnificent natural attractions right on the edge of the city centre. Away from town things get even better, with Rottnest Island, the Peel Region around Mandurah, the jarrah forests of the Perth Hills, and the beaches to the north all having a wealth of activity-based attractions. Most of these places are within an hour's travelling time from Perth.

Perth (Map p128)

The city's major recreational playgrounds include the Swan River – an outstanding feature of the metropolitan area – and a string of stunning ocean beaches. A refuge for native wildlife as well as stressed city-dwellers, Kings Park features a significant remnant of native bush on the edge of the central business district. Rottnest Island is a very popular summer destination and offers a variety of outdoor activities.

Things to do in and around Perth include a range of water sports (scuba diving, snorkelling, swimming, surfing, windsurfing and fishing are all popular). Among other things, you can cycle along the coast and rivers, take a whale-watching cruise, go canoeing and sea kayaking, watch birds in urban wetlands, bushwalk and, in the Swan Valley, sample some great wines.

Swan River (Maps pp128, 115, 116)

Known for most of its length as the Avon River, the Swan enters Perth's greater metropolitan area about 50km from its mouth at the port of Fremantle. With 18km to go, it passes the city and enters a broad estuary, where it meets the Canning River. This large expanse of water forms the main focus for outdoor recreation. In its final stages the river becomes much narrower and space for leisure activities is restricted.

Cycling

Covering a total distance of about 95km, the scenic Around the Rivers Ride is one of Perth's outstanding cycling experiences. The ride takes you along the Swan and Canning rivers, for the most part following dual-use pathways close to the shore. It is broken into 12 sections, eight of which form a 60km looped return route along the Swan between the Causeway and Fremantle. A free brochure with detailed maps is available from BikeWest and local cycle shops.

Water Sports

The river has several pleasant swimming beaches with grassy picnic areas and shady trees to sit under. Good examples are **Point Walter** (in Bicton) and **Matilda Bay** (in Crawley), both of which have expansive lawns and easy access.

Windsurfing and kitesurfing are popular pastimes on the estuary, which has areas suitable for novices and advanced sailors alike. The most popular location is off the **Qantas Boat Landing** on the southern side of Pelican Point, an area noted for its crosswinds and large expanse of waist-deep water. You can rent windsurfing and kitesurfing gear from Pelican Point Wind Sports (✆ 08 9386 1830, 0414 386 184, www.pelican-windsurfing.com.au), which operates daily from the landing from the beginning of October to the end of April.

Another prime windsurfing location is **Lucky Bay**, adjacent to Applecross. The grassy foreshore along Melville Beach Rd is the main launching area for this area.

The estuary with its scenic surrounds and broad stretches of open water is an excellent venue for sailing. There are several yacht clubs based along the river, and they're often on the lookout for an extra pair of hands. Alternatively you can hire catamarans (and kayaks) from Fun Cats (✆ 0408 926 003, www.funcats.com.au), at the **Coode St jetty** in South Perth. They're on site daily from the beginning of September to the end of April.

In summer, canoeists can paddle the Swan River from its tidal limit about 5km down from the Upper Swan Bridge (on the Great Northern Hwy) to The Causeway, in Perth.

Manna from Heaven

Also known as blue swimmers, blue manna crabs *(Portunus pelagicus)* inhabit estuaries and inshore waters right around the South West coast. The Swan River, Cockburn Sound, Peel Inlet, Leschenault Inlet and Geographe Bay are all noted for their large populations of crabs. Each summer huge numbers are netted as part of the feeding frenzy that grips local fishers at this time.

Blue mannas are caught using drop nets from a boat or jetty, and scoop nets or hand-held wire hooks while wading in the shallows. The minimum size across the broadest part of the carapace is 127mm, and a bag limit of 20 crabs per person (40 per boat) applies. All under-sized or egg-carrying crabs must be returned to the water immediately.

To cook the crabs, boil them for eight minutes and leave in the cooling water for 10 minutes. Cool rapidly under the tap – and start eating. Enjoy!

Fishing

Visiting anglers will find plenty of opportunities for shore and jetty fishing along the Swan River. Each spot seems to have its own suite of species, but generally there's a reasonable chance of catching black bream, cobbler, flathead, flounder and tailor, with mulloway an outside chance at night. Blue manna crabs get plenty of attention in summer.

Coastal Beaches (Maps pp128, 114)

If you're in Perth during summer you'll probably be keen to check its beautiful ocean beaches, particularly **Cottesloe** with its cafes, pubs and lively social scene. Long stretches of dazzling white sand line the coast from Fremantle in the south to **Quinns Rocks** in the north, a distance of about 45km. Most are safe for swimming, but there are dangerous rips and shore dumps in places. The more popular beaches are patrolled by surf life-savers from the beginning of October to the end of March – observe warning signs and stay between the red-and-yellow flags. See the Beach Updates section at www.mybeach.com.au.

Cycling

A shared pathway hugs the coast between **Woodmans Point** in the south and **Burns Beach** in the north. The ride covers a total distance of about 50km broken into eight sections, each of which is described in a free brochure called *Ride Along the Sunset Coast*. It's available from BikeWest and local cycle shops.

Beaches for Naturists

Perth's only nude beach is at **Swanbourne**, the next beach north from Cottesloe. To get there, walk up the beach from the car park at the northern end of Marine Parade.

Diving & Snorkelling

Some good scuba-diving and snorkelling spots are along the metropolitan coast between **Safety Bay** in the south and Mindarie in the north. These include the **Shoalwater Islands Marine Park** (adjacent to Safety Bay, in Rockingham), **Carnac Island** (off Coogee), and the **Marmion Marine Park** (adjacent to Hillarys). The marine parks include extensive seagrass beds and eroded limestone reefs, the latter featuring spectacular underwater topography with an abundance of marine life. Sea lions and bottlenose dolphins are often seen in Shoalwater Bay and around Carnac. Visibility is usually around 10m, but can be twice that on a good day.

Dive operators visiting these areas include Bell Scuba (Rockingham), Scubanautics (Rockingham) and Sorrento Quay Dive Shop (Hillarys). For contact details see Diving & Snorkelling pp38-39.

Fishing

Fishing is an extremely popular pastime and there are numerous worthwhile spots to do it in. Tailor prefers white water and is a much sought-after species in summer along surf beaches and groynes at places like **Cottesloe**, **Scarborough** and **Sorrento**. The reef holes at **Burns Beach** are famous for their big tailor; **Trigg Blue Holes** is another top spot for tailor and, in autumn, salmon. Herring and whiting are common catches right along the coast, and there's always the chance of a mulloway. The Swan River mouth is protected by the **North** and **South Moles** – two huge walls of rock that attract big fish like mulloway and snapper. It's a good spot for salmon in season and tailor; other common species include flathead, flounder, herring and tarwhine.

Sea Kayaking

The combination of sheltered waters, small islands and wildlife makes **Shoalwater Bay**, in the Shoalwater Islands Marine Park, a great spot for kayaking. An easy and enjoyable day trip takes you from **Point Peron** south to **Penguin Island** and return, passing close to limestone reef platforms and **Bird**, **Seal** and **Shag** islands. You can view the sea-bird rookeries and sea lions en route, but landing is only permitted on Penguin Island (see the boxed text). Another option is to paddle from Point Peron to Penguin Island, then catch the ferry back to the mainland.

Capricorn Kayak Tours (© 1800 625 688, www.capricornkayak.com.au) and Rivergods both offer full-day kayaking trips on Shoalwater Bay.

Surfing

Due to the sheltering influence of Garden and Rottnest islands and various reefs, there is little surf to the south of Fremantle. North of Freo, however, some beaches are better known for surfing and windsurfing than swimming.

The surf along the coast here could be described as more recreational than challenging. Even so, you'll often find good breaks at Cottesloe, **South Swanbourne**, Scarborough and **Trigg**. The artificial surf reef between **Leighton** and Cottesloe only works in a large swell, of which there aren't many. Cottesloe is closed to surfers from September to March.

For surf and weather reports, tune to 92.9 on your FM dial. Forecasts can be found on the various websites that deal with such matters (e.g. www.coastaloutlook.com.au and www.coastaldata.com).

Swimming with Dolphins

The waters off Rockingham, 25km south of Fremantle, are home to 100 or more bottlenose dolphins, and the prospect of being able to interact with them in their own environment is a major local attraction (see Swimming with Marine Mammals pp36-37). The CALM-approved tour operator is Rockingham Dolphins (© 08 9591 1333, www.dolphins.com.au); 'dolphin swim' tours run daily from the beginning of September to the end of May and cost $155. You can do a 'dolphin watch' boat tour if you don't want to get wet.

The friendly and informative Rockingham Visitor Centre (© 08 9592 3464) at 43 Kent St has details of all local wildlife tours.

Discovering Penguins

Just 700m off Mersey Point in Rockingham, south of Perth, 12.5ha Penguin Island is basically a lump of limestone and sand covered in low scrub. Yet this unprepossessing place is home to a variety of wildlife including Western Australia's largest breeding colony of little penguins (*Eudyptula minor*). About 1200 penguins – as well as other sea birds such as silver gulls and bridled terns – breed here each year.

Penguin Island is managed by CALM, which runs the Penguin Island Discovery Centre. Here interpretive signs tell you all about these fascinating birds, a number of which can be observed as they go about their business in a nocturnal house and recreated marine habitat.

Penguin Island is closed to the public during the breeding season (usually from June to about September). Otherwise a ferry plies back and forth between Mersey Point and the island on the hour from 9am to 4pm each day. Tickets cost $13.50 return including entry to the discovery centre.

For information on the island, contact Penguin & Seal Island Cruises (© 08 9528 2004, www.pengos.com.au), which operates the ferry. It also offers nature-based cruises from Penguin Island to other islands in Shoalwater Bay. These tours include a glass-bottom boat ride to Seal Island and a snorkelling cruise that takes in Bird and Seal islands.

There's an excellent underwater trail along a shallow reef on Pelican Island's southern side. It features a rich variety of marine life and is perfect for snorkelling.

Perth & Surrounds

Windsurfing & Kitesurfing

South of Fremantle, **Woodmans Point** and **Safety Bay** offer good conditions for windsurfing and kitesurfing. Heading northwards, Leighton, Cottesloe, Scarborough and **Pinaroo Point** (in Hillarys) are popular windsurfing places. None of the places mentioned north of Freo are considered suitable for novices.

SOS Surf Company (☎ 08 9430 7050) at 1 Quarry St, Fremantle, rents out kitesurfing boards and windsurfing equipment. Go Windsurfing (☎ 0438 853 785, www.gowindsurfing.com) rents windsurfing gear and holds clinics on the foreshore near the intersection of Safety Bay Rd and Waimea Rd, in Rockingham. They're on site daily from the beginning of October to the end of March.

Parks & Gardens

The metropolitan area has a number of bush parks, most of which are centred on wetlands. Many of these are ideal for bird-watching, walking and picnicking in natural surroundings.

Kings Park (Map p128, F3)

One of Perth's favourite outdoor areas, Kings Park is 404ha of bushland, parklands and botanic garden right on the city's doorstep. Native bush dominated by eucalypts, banksias and she-oaks covers more than two-thirds of the park. The city's founders have left a remarkable legacy, as no other Australian capital has such a large, relatively unspoilt area of original vegetation adjoining its central business district.

For visitor information on this unique park, contact ☎ 08 9480 3634 or check the website www.bgpa.wa.gov.au. The park's information centre is on Fraser Ave, just inside the park's main entrance.

Kings Park can be explored on a network of shared cycling/walking pathways – bikes are available for rental near the information centre – and there's a 600m elevated walkway near the Water Garden. This is a highlight of the park, but note that it is *not* a treetop walk. The superb views of the city centre and Swan River on offer at lookout points along Forrest Drive are a major attraction.

The bush is home to around 450 plant species as well as numerous small mammals and reptiles. In spring the native vegetation bursts into bloom in time to complement the popular **Kings Park Wildflower Festival**, held each year in September.

Guided walks (free) take place daily at 10am and 2pm and last from one to three hours, depending on the walk. There are four walks including a tour of the 17ha **Western Australian Botanic Garden**, which features many examples of the state's unique flora. Other walks explore the park's heritage and its native bushland. Self-guided walking tours of the botanic garden and adjacent bush are also available.

Bold Park (Map p128, F1-F2)

Covering 437ha of consolidated sandhills 8km west of the Perth CBD, Bold Park is one of the largest patches of native bush remaining in the metropolitan area. The park has a diverse range of vegetation communities dominated by tuart and banksia woodlands. A total of 266 native plant species and 81 native birds have been recorded, and you can see many of them from the park's extensive network of walking tracks. Other features include the views from **Reabold Hill** at 93m above sea level, this vegetated dune is the highest natural point on the Swan Coastal Plain. **Camel Lake**, so called because it was once a camel quarantine area, is the focus of a 1.8km heritage trail that winds through jarrah and marri in the park's east.

For information on Bold Park, contact ☎ 08 9387 0800 between 10am and 2pm weekdays or check the Kings Park website.

Swan Estuary Marine Park (Map p128, G2-G3)

This 325ha park consists of three separate reserves at **Alfred Cove** (adjacent to the suburbs of Applecross and Attadale), **Pelican Point** (adjacent to Crawley) and **Milyu**, which abuts the Kwinana Freeway opposite Pelican Point.

Perth CBD seen from Kings Park

The different segments all provide resting and feeding habitats for many bird species, and the park is of international significance by virtue of the estimated 10,000 migratory waders that visit from as far away as Siberia. Bird enthusiasts should find all three reserves worth visiting – Pelican Point has an observation tower.

Other Urban Wetlands

There are a number of other urban wetlands including the 266ha **Canning River Regional Park**, which stretches for about 5km along the river between Nicholson Rd and Riverton Bridge (on Fern Rd). This tranquil place has a wide diversity of habitats and is a good place to go bird-watching (97 recorded species), canoeing, fishing (for black bream), walking and cycling. Picnicking is popular at Kent St Weir and Masons Landing.

Another is the **Beeliar Regional Park** in Perth's southwest. This area incorporates two chains of wetlands where you'll find walking tracks, boardwalks, picnic facilities and many birds. North Lake and Bibra Lake are good spots to observe water birds, particularly in summer, while Thompson Lake is a stopping-off point for migratory waders. Booragoon Lake is an important breeding area for cormorants.

Star Swamp, in North Beach, has a 1.4km heritage walk that features a variety of vegetation communities and various points of historic interest. Just 6km from the CBD, **Herdsman Lake** is one of the best spots in the Perth region to observe water birds. This regional park has a wildlife-viewing centre, picnic facilities and cycling and walking tracks.

In the south, on Armadale Rd, **Forrestdale Lake** is a large, semipermanent body of water surrounded by a 245ha nature reserve. It's considered one of the South West's most important wetland habitats by virtue of the number and variety of water birds and migratory species that are seen here. There are plenty of bush birds, too.

Swan Valley Wineries
(Map p128, D6-B6)

The fertile soils of the Swan River Valley, on the Great Northern Hwy about 20km northeast from the Perth CBD, support a rich agricultural area in which wine grapes are the main crop. Grapes have been grown here since the 1830s, but it wasn't until 20 years later that the first commercial winery was established.

Today the valley has around 40 wineries with cellar doors scattered along the Great Northern Hwy between Midland, in the south, and the Swan River Bridge in the north. Most are small, family-owned concerns, which fosters a healthy sense of competition among wine makers. The most commonly produced varieties are chenin blanc, chardonnay, cabernet sauvignon and shiraz. The valley's hot summers are ideal for the production of fortified wines, with verdelho being particularly popular.

The Swan Valley & Guildford Tourist Information Centre (✆ 08 9379 9420, www.swanvalley.info) is on the corner of Meadow and Swan Sts in Guildford. Its friendly staff can advise you on the different options e.g. river cruises, horse-drawn cart – that are available for touring the local wineries and various other epicurean attractions.

The following places are not necessarily the best in the valley, but hopefully they'll give you an idea of what to expect:

- **Houghton Winery** – Dale Rd, Middle Swan. Established in 1859, historic Houghtons is probably best known for its white burgundy – a variety standard. This venerable complex has a pleasant alfresco eatery, a wine-making museum and an art gallery. A large grassed area with shady trees and toilet facilities makes a popular setting for family picnics.
- **Lamont's Winery** – Bisdee Rd, Millendon. Lamont's produces a good range of wines but its outstanding attraction is food. The meals served in its pleasantly situated restaurant and alfresco eatery – try the platter-style lunches – are pricey but delicious. Marron (a large freshwater crayfish) is a speciality of the restaurant.
- **Talijancich Wines** – Hyem Rd, Herne Hill. The main attraction here is an excellent muscat.
- **Sittella Winery** – Barrett St, Herne Hill. This winery on an attractive hilltop setting produces some excellent wines from local grapes including the easy-drinking Silk (a blended verdelho-chenin blanc-chardonnay) and Satin (a cab sav-shiraz-merlot). It has an up-market restaurant.
- **Swan Valley Wines** – Haddrill Rd, Baskerville. Owned by the friendly

Hoffman family, this small winery produces a range of wines including fruit wines and a delicious chocolate port.

- **Duckstein Brewery** – West Swan Rd, Henley Brook. This German-style microbrewery is one of four boutique breweries in the valley. It produces a range of full-flavoured brews including a good porter and several wheat beers. In summer, try its classic pilsener.

Rottnest Island (Map p114, D4-D5)

Lying 18km off the Perth coast, Rottnest Island (affectionately known as "Rotto") is one of Perth's most popular summer playgrounds. The island, which is formed mainly of limestone, measures 11km long by 4.5km at its widest point. Most of the facilities are centred on the little settlement of Thomson Bay, at the island's eastern end.

The Dutch explorer Willem de Vlamingh went ashore here in 1696 and saw many 'rats' and their nests (hence *Rottenest*, later modified to Rottnest). Actually the 'rats' were quokkas – small, wallaby-like marsupials that are still common on the island.

First settled in 1831, Rotto features some of Australia's oldest surviving streetscapes and architecture. Its fascinating if chequered history includes a brutal period as an Aboriginal penal settlement, and there are many relics of that time – a lot of the old buildings were constructed by Aboriginal prisoners. Used as an internment camp in both world wars, it was fortified with heavy guns in the late 1930s as part of Western Australia's coastal defences. The complex has been restored and is now a military museum.

Information

The visitor information centre (☎ 08 9372 9780, www.rottnest.wa.gov.au) is in Thomson Bay, a short walk from the main jetty.

Getting There

Rottnest Air Taxi (☎ 08 9292 5027, rottnestair@optusnet.co.au) flies to Rotto from Jandakot airport. Flights cost from $40 one-way and from $66 return.

Alternatively, take a sea ferry from Perth, Fremantle or Hillarys:

- **Boat Torque Cruises** – from Barrack St in Perth (☎ 08 9221 5844), C Shed in Fremantle (☎ 08 9335 6406) and Northport (☎ 08 9430 5844)
- **Hillarys Fast Ferries** – from Hillarys Boat Harbour (☎ 08 9246 1039)
- **Oceanic Cruises** – from Barrack St in Perth (☎ 08 9325 1191) and B Shed, Fremantle (☎ 08 9335 2666)
- **Rottnest Express** – from C Shed, Fremantle (☎ 08 9335 6406)

The ferry ride takes about 30 minutes from Fremantle ($45 return), 45 minutes from Hillarys ($60 return) and 100 minutes from Perth ($60 return). All operators will carry bikes ($10 return) and kayaks ($15 return).

The cheapest way to get there, other than paddling a kayak, is to take part in the Rottnest Island Channel Swim, held in February.

Getting Around

There are no rental cars on Rottnest, so away from Thomson Bay you'll have to hop on a bus, ride a bicycle or walk. Bikes can be rented from Rottnest Island Bike Hire (☎ 08 9292 5105) next to the Rottnest Hotel. Roads on the island are sealed and the slopes are generally easy.

The Bayseeker Bus does regular runs around the island and passengers can get on or off at any stop.

What to See & Do

Rotto is a major stronghold of one of Australia's many rare and endangered mammal species, the quokka. These cute little marsupials are a common sight around Thomson Bay, where they have a habit of hopping up to visitors in the hope of being fed. Try to resist, as feeding them will render you liable to an on-the-spot fine. Ask at the visitor centre about the free quokka tours.

Also of interest to wildlife enthusiasts are the migratory waders that congregate on the island's lakes in summer.

Arriving on a hot summer's day, you'll take one look at the clear turquoise water and brilliant white sandy beach at Thomson Bay and experience a mad urge to plunge in. There are lots of safe swimming spots around the coast, but be warned that stingers can be a problem on the northern beaches from **Natural Jetty** west to **Little Armstrong Bay**. See the section on Swimming p36.

At first glance Rotto doesn't look like a prime surfing location, but around on the unprotected backside of the island are some great breaks. You'll find 11 of the best described on the *Rottnest Island Surf Map*, available at the visitor centre.

Perth & Surrounds

They include **Strickland Bay**, a powerful left and right-hander that forms the venue for two state events in May. Surfboards and body-boards can be hired from Rottnest Malibu Dive (℗ 08 9292 5111).

Fishing is a popular pastime and there are numerous reefs and beaches worth trying. A good spot to cast a line near the settlement is **Natural Jetty**, where herring, King George whiting, skippy and tailor are common catches. Further west, **Salmon Bay** is one of the island's best places for shore fishers – a variety of species including herring, mulloway, salmon (in autumn), skippy, and King George whiting are caught here. Rottnest Malibu Dive rents fishing gear and sells bait.

Snorkelling along the island's south coast reveals a profusion of tropical fish (around 100 species) and coral growths (20 species) – compare this to the 11 species of tropical fish found in the colder waters along the metropolitan coast. This diversity is due to the Leeuwin Current (see p40). **Salmon Point**, **Little Salmon Bay** and **Parker Point** – all on the peninsula that separates Salmon Bay from Porpoise Bay – are outstanding and are protected within a marine sanctuary. If you're keen to explore further afield, check the excellent *Snorkeller's Guide to Rottnest Island*, by Dr Barry Hutchins, available from the visitor centre, which describes 60 underwater trails suitable for snorkelling. Underwater Explorer (℗ 0400 202 340, www.underwaterexplorer.com) does 90-minute snorkelling tours costing $22.

The next step up from snorkelling is to go hookah diving with Power Dive (℗ 0439 668 265, www.powerdive.com), based at **Pinkys Beach** next to the Bathurst Lighthouse. With the hookah system you use a floating air supply instead of carrying compressed air in a tank on your back. All dives are supervised – unless you have a diver's certificate – and the tour (from $40) includes a 20-minute orientation.

Scuba diving is extremely popular in the waters around Rotto, where eroded limestone reefs feature a range of spectacular topography and a wealth of marine life. There are many good dive sites, including a number of wrecks. Rottnest Malibu Dive (℗ 08 9292 5111) does shore and boat dives, and has a full range of scuba equipment for hire. Numerous dive operators visit the area from Perth.

Jetty fishing at Thomson Bay

A fun way to view the underwater world without getting your feet wet is to hire an electric-powered, two-person, glass-bottomed boat. These unusual little craft are available from Time Out (℗ 0413 181 322) at Geordie Bay ($18 per boat for 30 minutes). Alternatively, do a 45-minute tour with Underwater Explorer costing $18/49 for adults/families.

The Rottnest Island coast with its many rocky headlands and secluded beaches is ideal for sea kayaking. If you haven't brought your own craft you can hire one from Capricorn Kayak Tours (℗ 1800 625 688, www.capricornkayak.com.au). It also offers guided trips that last from two hours to a full day.

Last but by no means least of Rotto's water sports is sailing. You can tool around on the sheltered waters of Thomson Bay in a surf-cat rented from Rottnest Surfcat Hire (℗ 0415 965 947), based at the Army Jetty in Thomson Bay South.

Where to Stay

The Rottnest Island Authority (℗ 08 9432 9111) administers camping and self-contained units – its accommodation office is at the end of the main jetty. Other options include:

- Kingstown Barracks Youth Hostel –
  ℗ 08 9292 5999
- Rottnest Hotel – ℗ 08 9292 5011
- Rottnest Lodge – ℗ 08 9292 5161

Perth Hills (Map p115)

Formed by uplift along the eastern side of the Darling Fault, the Darling Range (or Perth Hills) southeast of Perth provides a scenic backdrop to the metropolitan area. Much of this area is contained within the 35,000ha Darling Range Regional Park and several national parks and state forests.

Walking and cycling are major activities, with many excellent routes to choose from. These include the long-distance Bibbulmun Track and Munda Biddi Trail, both of which have their northern terminuses here. The **Kep Track** is a shared path that, when completed, will link Mundaring Weir to Northam, about 60km east – the 20km section from the weir to Mt Helena is open, and the next 20km is due for completion in late 2004. Another major walking/cycling route is the 70km **Railway Reserve Heritage Trail**, which retraces the old Eastern Railway between Midland and Wooroloo. The 27km **Kattamordo Heritage Trail** links Mundaring with Bickley Reservoir, near Lesmurdie on the eastern fringe of the metropolitan area.

Wungong Gorge and Bungendore Park, both within the Darling Range Regional Park, are magnets for bird-watchers keen to observe endemics. Granite and dolerite outcrops (e.g. Churchmans Brook) and quarry faces (e.g. Boya Quarry near Boya, and Stratham Quarry at **Gooseberry Hill**) attract abseilers and climbers. Other attractions include dams and wineries.

The Mundaring Visitor Centre (☎ 08 9295 0202) at 7225 Great Eastern Hwy has a good range of leaflets on local walks and cycling routes. Also in Mundaring, CALM's district office (☎ 08 9295 1955) is on Mundaring Weir Rd.

Walyunga National Park
(Map p115, B7-B8)

About 40km northeast of Perth via the Great Northern Hwy, Walyunga National Park covers 1800ha of rugged, deeply incised valley near the foot of the Darling Range. It includes a long stretch of the Avon River, and was the site of one of the region's largest traditional Nyoongar camps. Conditions for walking and enjoying the wildflowers are best in September.

For information, contact the ranger on ☎ 08 9571 1371, or try CALM's Mundaring office.

What to See & Do

Walyunga has several walking tracks up to 10.6km in length. One that everyone can do is the **Aboriginal Heritage Trail** (600m one-way), which follows the Avon River between Walyunga Pool and Boongarup Pool. Signs along the way introduce creation stories of the Nyoongar people as well as traditional use of plants and animals. The walk along the river to **Syd's Rapids** and return (5.2km) is mostly a

pleasant ramble under shady gums, with wildlife usually a highlight early or late in the day. There's also the **Kingfisher Walk Trail**, an 8.5km loop that features the varied flora of the Darling Ranges.

In winter the Avon's character within the park changes from a string of quiet pools to a succession of raging white-water rapids. These form part of the annual **Avon Descent**, which takes place in early August (see Northam p99). Syd's Rapids are classified as grade three. The section of river from Walyunga downstream to Bells Rapids offers exciting white-water rafting.

Avon Valley National Park
(Map p115, A8-B8)

About 60km northeast of Perth, this 4400ha park on the Avon River lies in the transition zone between jarrah forests in the west and wandoo woodlands in the east. It sees few visitors compared to John Forrest National Park and is a good spot in which to get away from it all.

Access is via Morangup Rd, which turns off Toodyay Rd about 42km from Midland. The park's internal roads are unsealed and steep – definitely not recommended for caravans.

For information, contact CALM's district office in Mundaring (☎ 08 9295 1955).

What to See & Do

The main activity here is bush camping, with four areas available. The Bald Hill Campsite offers views of the granite outcrops that line the rugged Avon River valley, while the Valley Campsite is a good launch spot for canoes.

The diversity of plant communities makes this park a particularly good spot to see wildflowers.

John Forrest National Park
(Map p115, C8)

This 2700ha park, named after a famous Western Australian explorer and politician, lies within the northern jarrah forest on the crest of the Darling Scarp. Just 25km east of Perth, this was the state's first national park. It is readily accessible on sealed roads leading off the Great Eastern Highway, and is a popular destination for day visitors from Perth – park facilities include a tavern and tea rooms.

For information, contact the ranger on ☎ 08 9298 8344.

What to See & Do

The main-use area has several picnic and barbecue spots near a small dam on Jane Brook – a good spot for bird-watching on a quiet day.

There are a number of walking tracks including the **Eagle's Trail Walk**, a 15km circuit through the park's remote northern half. The many highlights en route include picturesque wandoo woodland, great views and a wonderful sense of isolation. Walkers are required to register their intentions at the ranger's office.

For something less challenging, the Railway Reserve Heritage Trail runs through the park close to the northern side of Jane Brook – this section includes WA's only railway tunnel and provides access to two attractive seasonal waterfalls, **National Park Falls** and **Hovea Falls**. The 2km walk from the picnic area to **Glen Brook Dam** is also recommended.

Paruna & Karakamia Sanctuaries

The Darling Range has two significant wildlife sanctuaries owned by a not-for-profit environmental organisation called the Australian Wildlife Conservancy (© 08 9572 3169, www.australianwildlife.org). Visitors are welcome, but you must book prior to arrival.

Paruna Sanctuary

The 2000ha Paruna Sanctuary is a wildlife corridor that links Walyunga and Avon Valley national parks (Map p115, B8). Stretching about 10km along the south bank of the Avon River, it is mostly in pristine condition and features great views, seasonal waterfalls and wildflowers. Paruna can be explored on a network of walks (each of which is covered by an excellent brochure) that vary in length from 2.3km to 13.4km. The longest walk is a tough slog on steep slopes in places, but is well worth the effort. Entry costs $5 per walker.

Karakamia Sanctuary

Near Chidlow (Map p115, C9), the Karakamia Sanctuary features a broad diversity of major habitats including jarrah, marri and wandoo woodlands, granite outcrops, heathlands and a permanent lake. These may be explored on two walking tracks that take around two hours to complete. A number of native mammal species have been reintroduced into a compound

surrounded by 9km of vermin-proof fence, and these can be seen on a guided dusk tour ($15/40 per adult/family); a minimum of eight applies.

Mundaring (Map p115, C8)

On the Great Eastern Hwy 35km east of Perth, this small township is a good base from which to explore local conservation reserves and the various cycling and walking routes that cut through the area.

The Mundaring Visitor Centre (© 08 9295 0202) at 7225 Great Eastern Hwy has a good range of leaflets on local walks and cycling routes. CALM's district office (© 08 9295 1955) is on Mundaring Weir Rd.

What to Do

Attractions in the area include beautiful **Lake Leschenaultia,** a man-made reservoir set in jarrah/marri forest near Chidlow, about 50km from Perth. The activities available here include walking (9km of tracks), canoeing (Canadians for hire), swimming, picnicking and camping. There's often live music on summer weekends. Contact © 08 9572 4248 for more details.

The **Hills Forest Discovery Centre** (© 08 9295 2244) on Mundaring Weir Rd runs seasonal programmes of nature-based activities for all ages. These can include guided walks, Aboriginal culture tours, close encounters with native animals and wildflower walks. Bookings are essential.

Where to Stay

There are several places to stay around Mundaring, including:

- Djaril Mari YHA Hostel – © 08 9295 1809
- Lake Leschenaultia – © 08 9572 4248 (tents only)
- Mundaring Caravan Park – © 08 9295 1125
- Mundaring Weir Hotel – © 08 9295 1809

North of Perth

The coastal plain to the north of Perth has two of WA's best-known national parks (Nambung and Yanchep) as well as great wildflower-viewing in spring. Between them, the little coastal settlements of Guilderton, Lancelin and Cervantes offer a range of outdoor pursuits – Lancelin is renowned as a national windsurfing centre.

Perth & Surrounds

Yanchep National Park
(Map p114, A5)

On the Swan Coastal Plain just 50km from the city centre, the 2842ha Yanchep National Park features a variety of significant habitats such as limestone caves, freshwater swamps and lakes, heath and eucalypt woodlands. Yanchep comes from *yanget*, the Nyoongar name for the bulrushes that grow so prolifically in the wetlands here. The roots were a major traditional food source.

The holiday township of Grey in the distance, on the 4WD coastal track between Lancelin and Cervantes

This attractive and popular park also boasts a large koala enclosure, stunning (in season) wildflower gardens and grassy lakeside picnic areas. The main developed area contains several charming 1930s Tudor-style buildings including a museum, a pub (the Yanchep Inn) and tearooms.

Guided cave tours and Nyoongar Aboriginal culture tours are conducted daily. Over 400 caves have been found in this area, but only two (Crystal Cave and Yonderup Cave) are open to the public. Adventure caving is available, but only to school groups and the like.

Wanneroo Rd (State Hwy 60) cuts through the park en route between Perth and Lancelin.

The visitor information centre (✆ 08 9561 1004) opens daily between 9.15am and 4.30pm.

What to Do

Bird-watching can be a rewarding pastime as the park's varied habitats attract a diversity of birdlife, including several WA endemics including the endangered Carnaby's black-cockatoo. The wildflowers are always popular, particularly in September when the extensive heathlands are in full bloom – a fantastic sight.

Walkers can explore the park and its surrounds on a number of marked trails, all of which are shown on maps available from the visitor centre. They range from short (an hour or less) habitat walks to more challenging day and longer excursions.

The latter include the 19.5km **Yanchep Rose Trail**, which, from early July to late August, features the spectacular yet intriguing blooms of the Yanchep rose. Other attractions are great views and WWII radar bunkers. Another is the 27.5km **Yaberoo Budjara Trail**, which offers stunning views and follows the traditional route of the local Nyoongar people as they travelled between the lakes.

Lancelin (Map p110, F3)

This small coastal resort town and crayfishing port is about 125km from Perth at the northern end of the sealed coast road (State Hwy 60) through Yanchep National Park. It's a windy place, which has helped it become one of Australia's main windsurfing centres.

A 4WD track continues up the coast to meet the Cervantes-Pinnacles Desert Road about 63km from Lancelin. En route you cross a bombing range, drive 7km along a beach and negotiate hazards such as corrugations, rocks and soft dunes. Travel the beach only at low tide (get tide-times from *The West Australian* newspaper) and allow at least four hours for the overall trip. Note that tyre deflation is essential north of the fishing village of Wedge.

Driving up from Perth you pass the turn-off to the tiny coastal holiday-ville of **Guilderton**, at the mouth of the Moore River. Outdoor pursuits available here include fishing (beach and estuary), scuba diving, canoeing and bird-watching.

Information

Lancelin's visitor information centre is at 102 Gingin Rd (✆/fax 08 9655 1100). Ask here for details (including a mud map) of the coastal track to Cervantes.

What to Do

For such a quiet, unprepossessing little place Lancelin certainly has a lot of things to do in the outdoor pursuits department. The town's major attraction is windsurfing, which mainly takes place between mid-November and the end of April. Werner's Hot Spot (✆ 08 9655 1553, 0407 426 469, www.auswind.com.au)

operates from the beach at the end of Hopkins St. Werner hires windsurfing and kitesurfing gear, and gives tuition. Each year the town hosts the **Lancelin Ocean Classic** (see Windsurfing pp40-41).

There are good surfing breaks on reefs in the area, the best being off **Back Beach**. Adrift Surfing (✆ 08 9403 5726, 0410 774 132, www.adriftsurfing.com) runs all-inclusive day and overnight learn-to-surf tours from Perth to Lancelin and nearby Wedge Island.

Lancelin is on a sheltered bay with glorious white sand beaches and safe swimming from one end to the other. Swimmers often find themselves sharing the water with dolphins, while sea lions also pop up from time to time.

There's good snorkelling on the reefs around **Edward Island** (best at low tide) and in the fish habitat-protected area behind **Lancelin Island**. A string of 14 wrecks dating from 1656 to 1983 attracts scuba divers to the coast between Lancelin and Guilderton, 40km south. They are described in the WA Maritime Museum's excellent brochure, *Shipwrecks of the Guilderton to Lancelin Coast*.

Beach fishing isn't a huge attraction, but wetting a line can be fruitful off the jetty (squid) and in the channel between the mainland and Edward Island (herring, whiting and cobbler). In March the channel is a hot spot for tailor.

In spring and early summer, **bird-watching** is a rewarding pastime on Lancelin and Edward islands, both of which are wildlife sanctuaries. A number of sea-bird species including ospreys and several terns nest there – walk only on established paths to avoid stepping on the nests. Lancelin Island is home to a rare red-legged skink and also has a small colony of sea lions.

The huge, white, Sahara-like dunes behind Lancelin make a good venue for **sand boarding**. Boards can be hired from the Have a Chat Supermarket and the Surf & Sports Shop, both on Gingin Rd near the information centre. Board hire ranges from $10 to $14 per hour.

You can also explore the dunes on a quad or two-wheeled off-road motorcycle. Pinnacle Tours (✆ 0417 919 550) offers guided tours, or you can hire the bikes and do your own thing. Bike/quad hire costs $75/85 per hour.

Where to Stay

The information centre is the booking agent for numerous short-term rental properties in Lancelin and Ledge Point. Other options include:

- Ledge Point Caravan Park –
  ✆ 08 9655 1066
- Lancelin Caravan Park – ✆ 08 9655 1056
- Lancelin Lodge YHA – ✆ 08 9655 2020,
  www.lancelinlodge.com.au
- Lancelin Hotel Motel – ✆ 08 9655 1005,
  lancelininn@bigpond.com
- Windsurfer Beach Chalets –
  ✆ 08 9655 1454

DENIS O'BYRNE

The Moore River mouth at Guilderton

Cervantes & Nambung National Park (Map p110, C2-C3-D2)

On the Swan Coastal Plain 245km north of Perth, Cervantes is a small resort town and crayfishing port near the northern end of the 17,500ha Nambung National Park at the park's northern end. The Jurien Bay Marine Park stretches north along the coast from Wedge Island (between Cervantes and Lancelin) to Green Head.

Information

The Cervantes Visitor Centre (✆ 08 9652 7700) is next to the shops on Iberia St. Ask here for a mud map and route information if taking the coastal track south to Lancelin – see the earlier section on that town.

Nambung is managed from the CALM office in Cervantes (✆ 08 9652 7043); contact its office in Jurien Bay on ✆ 08 9652 1911 for information on the marine park.

What to See & Do

Nambung National Park includes one of Western Australia's best-known tourist attractions: the **Pinnacles Desert**. Here you'll find strange, almost alien landscapes made up of hundreds of limestone pillars that rise eerily from the shifting yellow sands. The pillars, which are up to four metres high, are of all shapes and sizes. Some resemble giant Northern Territory termite mounds and others tombstones, while many could be bizarre modern sculptures. The end result is intriguing, to say the least.

A sealed road links the Pinnacles area with Cervantes, 17km distant, and there's a fee-collecting point at the end of the bitumen.

From here an unsealed vehicle track does a 4km circuit of the formations. You'll get the best appreciation of this fascinating area by leaving your vehicle in the car park and walking from there.

Beach fishing is popular at **Kangaroo Point** and **Hangover Bay**, both about 1km off the Pinnacles Desert road.

Cervantes is another popular windsurfing spot. Each year in early December it hosts the **Slalom Windsurfing Carnival**, which attracts local, interstate and international sailors.

Also of interest are the stromatolites of **Lake Thetis**, a short drive from town. As is usual in this part of the world, wildflowers are a major attraction in spring. The marine park has many good opportunities for scuba and snorkelling, not to mention fishing.

Where to Stay

Camping is not permitted in the national park, but Cervantes has several options including:

- Pinnacles Caravan Park – ✆ 08 9652 7060, cervpinncpark@westnet.com.au
- Pinnacles Beach Backpackers – bookings ✆ 1800 245 232, www.wn.com.au/pbbackpackers
- Cervantes Pinnacles Motel – ✆ 08 9652 7145, pinnacles@bigpond.com

Nambung National Park

One of the taller pillars of the Pinnacles

Other Parks

As well as Yanchep and Nambung, there are several other conservation areas between the Brand Hwy and the coast south of Cervantes. However, vehicle access to most is limited, none has any facilities and there is little reason to visit them other than the springtime wildflowers.

Badgingarra National Park (Map p110, B4) between Cervantes and the roadside hamlet of Badgingarra has a 3.5km walking track that leads to a lookout on the edge of a breakaway. The track starts opposite the Badgingarra Roadhouse, where you can park. For information contact CALM's Moora office on ℂ 08 9652 1911.

The 28,000ha **Julimar Conservation Park** (Map p111, J8-J9), 80km from Perth via the Great Northern and Brand highways, was once used for farming and timber production. Today, however, its wandoo woodlands and other habitats provide a refuge for a number of native mammal species that have been reintroduced as part of the Western Shield programme. There are no facilities and walking tracks, but you can explore the park by a network of narrow dirt roads suitable for 2WD vehicles – the best access is via Bindoon. For information contact CALM's district office in Mundaring on ℂ 08 9295 1955.

Peel Region

The Peel Region encompasses Mandurah and several small towns including Dwellingup, Jarrahdale, Mandurah, Pinjarra and Waroona. Within this area are the Murray River, the Peel Inlet, extensive jarrah forests and several national parks and nature reserves. There are good opportunities for bird-watching, bushwalking, canoeing and white-water rafting. Mandurah offers fishing and crabbing, and a chance to interact with dolphins. Other activities include horse rides (near Pinjarra) and bush camping.

Mandurah (Map p114, H6)

On Peel Inlet 75km south of Perth, Mandurah (pop 44,000) is a bustling coastal resort town and dormitory suburb for Perth. Activities of the watery kind are the main attractions here.

Information

The Mandurah Visitor Centre (ℂ 08 9550 3999, www.peeltour.net.au) is at 75 Mandurah Terrace. The CALM office (ℂ 08 9582 9333) is on Pinjarra Rd.

What to Do

Anyone keen on birds will get a kick out of Parrots of Bellawood Park (ℂ 08 9535 6732) at 64 Furnissdale Rd, Mandurah. Its **walk-in aviaries** house 49 native parrot species, several of which are rare and endangered.

The long white ocean beach between **Tims Thicket** (about 15km south of Mandurah) and the Harvey River mouth at **Myalup** is a great run in a 4WD vehicle. Note that headlands en route may not be passable at high tide. There's a short option at the northern end, where you can exit north of Seal Rock, otherwise the next exits are 24km away at **Preston Beach** and 46km away at Myalup. Fishing off the beach commonly yields whiting, herring and tailor.

The coast south of Mandurah is rapidly being smothered by suburbia, but fortunately the 12,900ha **Yalgorup National Park** preserves some of the natural environment. The park, which is in two parts, offers bush camping and walks. In the north, at **Lake Clifton**, a raised walkway gives a close-up view of a colony of thrombolites – ancient, rock-like structures built by micro-organisms that, like stromatolites, resemble the earliest forms of life on earth. Southwards, at **Lake Preston**, the 4.5km Heathland Walk is an absolute gem during the wildflower season. Ask for a brochure at the tourist centres in Mandurah or Waroona. The park contains an important remnant tuart forest, which unfortunately is in serious decline as a result of attack by eucalypt borers.

Mandurah's most famous attraction is probably the blue manna crabs that inhabit the Peel Inlet and **Harvey Estuary** (see the boxed text p44). Several places in town will rent you a boat suitable for crabbing; they'll also provide crab nets and (usually) bait. The visitor centre has details.

The wild **dolphins** that also live in the inlet form the basis of a nature-based tour operated by Dolphin Encounters (ℂ 0407 090 284). Their 'swimming with dolphins' excursion is approved by CALM and costs $140.

If you want to learn how to surf, **Secret Harbour** between Mandurah and Rockingham has ideal beginners' waves. Lets Go Surfing (ℂ 08 9537 3709) and Big Wave Surfing School (ℂ 08 9524 7671, www.bigwavesurfingschool .com) offer expert tuition.

While reasonable catches of fish can be made off local beaches and jetties, you need to go way out to really get among the action. For boat charters, see pp35-36.

There are several dive charters operating out of Mandurah. See Diving & Snorkelling pp38-39 for contact details.

Where to Stay

There are a large number of caravan parks in and around Mandurah:

- Aqua Caravan Park – ℂ 08 9535 1869
- Belvedere Caravan Park – ℂ 08 9535 1213
- Dawesville Caravan & Holiday Village – ℂ 08 9582 1417
- Lake Clifton Caravan Park – ℂ 08 9739 1255
- Settlers Estuary Caravan Park – ℂ 08 9534 2121
- Timbertop Caravan Park – ℂ 08 9535 1292
- Yalgorup Eco Park – ℂ 08 9582 1320, www.ecopark.com.au

Jarrahdale (Map p115, F8)

Established in the early 1870s, this declared historic town, 54km from Perth, was WA's first timber town. The Old Post Office on Jarrahdale Rd has details of numerous good walks to such diverse places as wetlands, virgin jarrah forest and the site of a 1940s POW camp – ask about the Jarrahdale Heritage Society's programme of guided walks.

Just west of town, **Serpentine National Park** features granite outcrops, jarrah/marri forest, heath and picturesque Serpentine Falls, the area's main scenic attraction. This is a good spot for bird-watching and walking – there are several tracks up to 11km return – and there's also a CALM campground just outside the park off Jarrahdale Rd.

Pinjarra (Map p114, H6)

On the scenic Murray River 86km from Perth, Pinjarra is far enough from the coast to avoid the summer mayhem of Mandurah.

The Pinjarra Tourist Centre (ℂ 08 9531 1438) on the corner of Henry and George Sts is the best source of information on the Peel Region outside Mandurah, particularly for outdoor activities. Its friendly staff can tell you about camping in the area, including bush sites.

What to Do

Canoeing is a popular activity in Pinjarra. The town is at the end of the Murray's tidal section, and from here it's 25km to the Peel Inlet – a good summer paddle.

On Drakes Brook just east of **Waroona**, a small township 26km south of Pinjarra, the Waroona Dam and Drakesbrook Weir are good for canoeing, trout fishing and marroning.

At the Harvey Estuary's southern end, about 16km southwest of Pinjarra, the forested **Kooljennup Nature Reserve** supports a diversity of native plants including several rare orchids. Also of interest here is the **Herron Point Walk** (or should that be wade?), which takes you across the estuary in the footsteps of the pioneers. This area is excellent for bird-watching: the islands and sandbars are often crowded with waders and water birds. You can also go camping, crabbing, prawning and swimming.

Organised Tours

Several operators do canoeing and white-water rafting trips on the Murray River. Dwellingup Adventures has some interesting options for self-guided overnight canoe trips. One of these involves a 13km walk on the Bibbulmun Track followed the next day by a 6km paddle – a great experience of the jarrah forest.

There are also a couple of places offering horse rides. Southeast of town off the Pinjarra-Williams Rd, Pioneer Trails of WA (ℂ 08 9581 1384, 0419 939 697, trails@southwest.com.au) has a variety of bush rides as does Langford Hill Riding Farm (ℂ 08 9733 1455) at Waroona.

Dwellingup (Map p115, J8)

This small timber-milling centre in the jarrah forest 110km south of Perth was burned to ashes in 1961, when a huge wildfire swept through the area. These days it is a hub for tourism. The Munda Biddi Trail and the Bibbulmun Track both pass through Dwellingup, and the popular Lane Poole Reserve is nearby.

Information

The Dwellingup History & Visitor Information Centre (ℂ 08 9538 1108, dhvic@wn.com.au) is on Marrinup St, while CALM's district office (ℂ 08 9538 1078) is on Banksiadale Rd.

In the Event of Fire

The downside of all those trees is the risk of a summer wildfire. Fortunately the chances of being caught in one are very small, particularly if you do the sensible thing and spend days of high fire danger at the beach. Fire warnings are broadcast on local radio stations. Otherwise contact CALM offices, shire offices and tourist information centres for advice on the current situation.

Here are some common-sense rules for walkers and motorists to follow in the unlikely event that they find themselves threatened by fire:

Walkers

- First and foremost, don't panic. Remain calm and try to determine where the fire is and which direction it's moving in.
- Move away from the fire by cutting across the slope – don't go uphill unless you know for certain that safety lies in that direction.
- Seek out large areas of low fuel (e.g. gravel pits or previously burned areas) in which to take refuge. Deep dams and streams are ideal but water tanks are not – they may rupture in the heat. Stay away from dense vegetation such as you find in gullies.
- Don't light a backburn – you may be caught up in the resulting wildfire.
- If the situation becomes dangerous, use whatever you can to protect yourself from radiant heat. Lie down in the shelter of a large rock or fallen log, preferably in a depression, and cover all exposed skin with dirt or whatever nonflammable material is at hand.
- Don't try to run through the flames unless they're less than a metre high and you can see what's on the other side.
- Drink plenty of water to prevent dehydration.

Motorists

It's important to realise that your vehicle can provide protection from a bushfire. Do not leave it unless you know for certain that safety is close at hand.

- If caught in a bushfire, stop immediately, preferably in a large, clear area. Do not attempt to drive through dense smoke or flames as you may worsen your situation by having an accident.
- Put your headlights on so that firefighters will be able to see you.
- Remove as much plastic and other synthetic materials as possible from the car – they may give off toxic fumes that force a premature exit.
- Close all windows, doors and vents, or switch the vents to recycle.
- Get down on the floor below window height and cover yourself with non-synthetic clothing or bedding (woollen blankets are perfect).
- The car will get very hot, but the fuel tank is unlikely to explode in the short time it will take for the fire front to pass – stay in the vehicle until it has.
- Drink plenty of water to prevent dehydration.

DENIS O'BYRNE

Perth & Surrounds

What to Do

The tourist office has details of numerous forest walks in the immediate area. A good short one is the 1.5km **Island Pool Trail**, in Lane Poole Reserve, which features granite outcrops, tall jarrah, grass trees and great views of the river and its valley.

On the edge of town on Acacia Rd, the **Forest Heritage Centre** (☎ 08 9538 1395, www.iinet .net.au/~fhc) has interpretive displays and trails, including an 11m-high 'canopy walk'. It's worth going there just to see the magnificent work on display in the Fine Wood Gallery.

The **South Dandalup Dam** 8km north of Dwellingup is a great spot for picnics and forest walks. However, all forms of water-based activities are prohibited as, like most other dams in this region, it supplies drinking water to Perth and other centres.

Just south of town, the 55,000ha **Lane Poole Reserve** features tall jarrah forest and a long stretch of the Murray River. In the reserve's northern section the river banks are dotted with campgrounds, picnic spots and canoe launching sites. Canoeing is a popular pastime within the reserve, particularly in spring when the floods have subsided and the days are getting warmer. In summer there are long pools suitable for paddling in the 10km between **Yarragil Campground** and the **Baden-Powell Waterspout**. In winter, novices can put their canoes in the water at Driver Rd and paddle the 36km to Baden-Powell Waterspout – the rapids beyond here should be left to the experts. Under no circumstances should beginners proceed beyond the ford at Scarp Pool, which marks the start of 10km of terrifying grade-four rapids.

Dwellingup Adventures (☎ 08 9538 1127) does tours in the area and has good-quality mountain bikes and canoes for hire.

Where to Stay

CALM manages several bush campgrounds along the Murray River in Lane Poole Reserve. Alternatively, try the following budget places in Dwellingup:

- Dwellingup Chalets & Caravan Park – ☎ 08 9538 1157
- Jarrah Forest Lodge – ☎ 08 9538 1395 ■

The Pinnacles – early morning or late afternoon bring out the best colours.

HENRY BOEGHEIM

Chapter Five

South West Corner

This diverse part of the South West has a beautiful coastline that stretches from north of Bunbury to Augusta and features long white beaches, sheltered coves and spectacular sea cliffs. In the hinterland are several national parks and reserves, numerous wineries and extensive jarrah forests. Between the trees and the beaches, the Swan Coastal Plain forms a broad arc north of Busselton. It has largely been cleared for agriculture, and some of WA's most productive farmland is found here.

Being just two hours drive on good roads from Perth it's not surprising that this whole area is a major weekend and holiday playground for city escapees. While forest communities remain quiet, the coastal resorts of Bunbury, Busselton, Dunsborough, Margaret River and Augusta burst at the seams on long weekends and the summer school holidays.

Bunbury Region

The Bunbury Region includes Bunbury (the South West's largest town after Albany and Mandurah) and several smaller towns such as Bridgetown, Collie and Nannup. The state forest around Nannup has some great walks, the Blackwood River is excellent for canoeing, and fishing and swimming are popular along the coast. Dolphins are a major attraction at Bunbury.

Bunbury (Map p118, E5)

This prosperous export-shipping terminal and regional centre (pop 28,000) lies on the shores of Geographe Bay, 184km from Perth. The town has several worthwhile activity-based attractions. The Bunbury Visitor Centre (℅ 1800 286 287, 9721 7922, www.bunburybreaks.com.au) in the old railway station on Carmody Place will be happy to tell you about them.

What to See & Do

The **Dolphin Discovery Centre** (℅ 08 9791 3088, www.dolphindiscovery.com.au) on Koombana Bay has excellent static and audio-visual displays that will tell you most things that you ever wanted to know about the local marine life. The main draw, though, is the wild bottlenose dolphins that regularly visit the centre to say g'day to their human admirers. This usually occurs between 8 and 11am, with up to 10 dolphins (and sometimes none) taking part. 'Dolphin swims', which are overseen by a marine biologist, take place on a daily basis (depending on the weather) from the beginning of November to the end of April – these take three hours and cost $99. Those who don't wish to get wet can observe the dolphins by taking a boat cruise from the centre ($30).

Scuba divers will want to visit the *Lena*, a Russian fishing vessel that was scuttled in December 2003 to form a dive wreck – it had been seized after being caught poaching fish in Australian waters. The wreck is 55m in length and sits upright in 18m of water about 5km off the coast. You can visit it with Bunbury Dive Charters (℅ 08 9721 1785) and Coastal Water Dive (℅ 08 9721 7786).

A couple of good spots for bird-watchers in the town area are the **mangrove boardwalk** opposite the Dolphin Discovery Centre, and **Big Swamp**, a permanent wetland that attracts many water birds and waders. Around 70 species of birds have been recorded at both places. The swamp has a 2km-long sealed path around it, and there's also a bird hide. As always, the best times are early or late in the day.

Koombana Bay and **Back Beach**, which has a small surfing break, offer safe swimming off white sandy beaches.

Just north of Bunbury, the **Leschenault Estuary** is popular with windsurfers and crabbers. The long and rather narrow **Leschenault Peninsula Conservation Park** has a bush campground, walking tracks and 4WD access to the beach, and it's another good spot for bird-watching, particularly water birds. Mozzie repellent is an absolute must here.

Dekked Out Adventures in Bunbury does sea-kayaking tours on the estuary. Along the way you'll learn to catch fish from your kayak, and meet some dolphins if your luck is in. They also have kayaks and canoes for rent.

To the east of town, the **Vasse-Wonnerup Wetland** is an internationally significant habitat for migratory birds – over 30,000 birds of more than 30 species visit the wetland each year.

Wellington Dam (Map p119, E7)

In the jarrah forest about 50km east of Bunbury, Wellington Dam on the Collie River supplies irrigation water to farms on the coastal plain. As water quality isn't the huge issue that it is for dams that supply domestic water to towns, the restrictions that occur else-where don't apply here.

The helpful staff at the Wellington Dam Café (℗ 08 9734 4274), on Weir Rd near the dam wall, can supply information on activities in the area.

What to Do

The café has rental canoes for lake and river trips – there are some long pools down-stream of the dam – and you can fish for red-fin perch and trout along the way. Adrenaline junkies can join a commercial tour and go white-water rafting from the dam wall down to **Honeymoon Pool**, a distance of about 6km. This is only possible in summer when water is released from the dam to recharge irrigation channels on the Swan Coastal Plain.

There are mountain-bike trails of varying lengths and grades of difficulty off River Road in the Mt Lennard area – ask at the café for directions. Alternatively you could cycle along forest roads from the café to **King Jarrah**, an impressive 3-500-year-old tree that somehow escaped the woodcutter's attentions. Look at its long, thick, straight trunk and the tree stumps scattered around on the open forest floor and you can easily picture what this area must have looked like before the introduction of steel axes.

For hikers, the 9.5km **Sika Circuit** leads from the café into mature jarrah forest, with views over the Collie River Valley en route. The walk is steep in parts and is easiest done in an anticlockwise direction. Nearby, in the **Wellington Discovery Forest**, two shorter trails have interpretive signage that explains something of the ecology of the jarrah forests.

Where to Stay

CALM has two great bush campgrounds near the dam wall – Potter's Gorge is by the lake, while Honeymoon Pool boasts a riverbank setting. Otherwise there's accommodation including a caravan park in the nearby coal-mining centre of Collie – check with the Collie Visitor Centre (℗ 08 9734 2051, www.collierivervalley.org.au) at 156 Throssell St.

Nannup & the Blackwood River (Map p122, A6)

The quaint timber town of Nannup is on the Blackwood River 59km southeast of Busselton. In summer this laid-back little place makes a refreshing change from the frenetic pace of nearby coastal resorts and the Margaret River area. Nannup has loads of character and you could easily spend a couple of days here discovering its various attractions.

The main outdoor activities in the area are bushwalking and canoeing, though fishing for trout and marron is also popular. One of the South West's most attractive drives links Nannup with Balingup (see Scenic Drives p30).

Information

The Nannup Visitor Centre (℗ 08 9756 1211, www.compwest.net.au/~nannuptb) is at the Busselton end of town, at 4 Brockman St. CALM's office (℗ 08 9756 1011) is on Warren Rd opposite the post office.

Walking

The highlight for bushwalkers is the 40km **Timberline Trail** between Nannup and Cambray Pool. This well-developed track, constructed on the alignment of a disued timber railway, follows St Johns Brook as it winds through the jarrah forest. It features historic relics of the logging days, and permanent water holes such as pretty **Barrabup Pool**. Check at the tourist office for the latest on bicycle access.

Alternatively, a 2km river walk takes you through riparian forest from the visitor centre to the **Blackwood River Winery**, which has tastings. The main street is just a few minutes' walk from the winery.

The state forest between the townships of Nannup, Bridgetown and Manjimup has a number of good walks. About 20km east of Nannup on the Brockman Hwy is the **Karri Gully** picnic area, an access point for the Bibbulmun Track. A little further on, **Bridgetown Jarrah Park** has a network of tracks along Maranup Creek – there are leaflets at the information shelter. Allow at least three hours walking time if you intend doing the lot.

On Sears Rd, which turns off the highway about 100m before the Bridgetown Jarrah Park intersection, the charming **Donnelly River Holiday Village** (℃ 08 9772 1244, www.donnelly-river-holiday-village.com.au) is a redeveloped mill settlement complete with a historic timber mill – and more forest walks.

Also in this general area, the **Willow Springs Campsite** on Golden Gully Rd (it turns off the highway between Karri Gully and Sears Rd) is another Bibbulmun Track access point. From here you can follow the track to **One Tree Bridge** as it winds through karri forest in the Donnelly River valley, a distance of 32km. See the section on Manjimup pp71-72.

Canoeing

The Blackwood is the largest of the South West's river systems and in winter it's possible to paddle all the way from Boyup Brook to the sea. However, most expeditions leave from Nannup as conditions upstream from there are often slow and difficult. It's 147km from Nannup to Hardy Inlet, with a further 9km across the estuary to meet the sea at Augusta.

You can canoe the entire river down from Nannup throughout the year. Log jams, tea-tree thickets and rapids abound, but even so, there's little requirement for portaging in winter and early spring. At other times you'll find yourself frequently stopping to lift the canoe over logs or drag it through shallow rapids.

Below Nannup the river flows mainly through uninhabited forest with numerous bush-camp sites en route. It becomes tidal a few km upstream of **Warner Glen** and is estuarine below **Molloy Island**.

Vehicle access points include **Darradup Bridge** (46km from Nannup), **Sues Bridge** (91km), **Great North Rd** (108km), Warner Glen Bridge (119km), **Alexandra Bridge** (133km) and **Molloy Island** (147km). These break the river up into stages that allow for a range of experiences from a day to a week – the most popular section is Sues Bridge to Warner Glen. Except at Darradup there are campgrounds either at or near all these places.

Make sure your canoe trip doesn't coincide with the **Blackwood Classic**, a powerboat race held in September between Bridgetown and Augusta. Ask at Bridgetown's tourist office for more information on this event.

You can hire canoes from Canoeing at Nannup (℃ 08 9756 1252) and Blackwood River Canoeing (℃ 08 9756 1209, blackwoodrivercanoeing@wn.com.au). The latter is on the river about 28km southwest of town via the Brockman Hwy.

Events

Nannup's gardeners are so committed to keeping their town looking good that each year they host several garden and flower festivals. The tourist office has full details.

Organised Tours

Blackwood River Canoeing specialises in guided and unescorted expeditions on the Blackwood. Unescorted expeditions cost from $35 per person per day. The two-hour 'twilight paddles' ($25 per person) from the beginning of November to the end of Easter are a great way to experience the river's unique atmosphere.

Where to Stay

There are numerous B&Bs, farmstays and the like in the Nannup area. For more basic accommodation, try:

- Nannup Caravan Park – ℃ 08 9756 1211, nannuptb@compwest.net.au
- Black Cockatoo Travellers Retreat – ℃ 08 9756 1035

Greenbushes & Bridgetown
(Map p119, H8-J8)

These small towns, just 16km apart, are on the South Western Hwy 79km and 95km respectively southeast of Bunbury. For information on this area, contact the Greenbushes Discovery Centre (℃ 08 9764 3883) on Blackwood Rd, and the Bridgetown Tourist Bureau (℃ 08 9761 1740, www.bridgetowntouristcentre.com.au) at 154 Hampton St.

Greenbushes has several forest walks and the discovery centre has details. The **Mining**

Heritage Walk (3km) is an interesting tour through jarrah forest, passing reminders of the early tin-mining days en route. The intriguingly named **New Zealand Gully Walk** (7km) also reveals the town's mining heritage. For a longer walk take the **Greenbushes Loop** (15km), which connects to the Bibbulmun Track.

Bridgetown is on the Blackwood River, and in winter experienced kayakers can ride the current all the way to the river's mouth. In summer there are several long pools suitable for canoeing near the town. Hire canoes are available from the Bridgetown Caravan Park (© 08 9761 1053) and Tall Timber Adventure Treks (© 08 9761 7076).

The tourist centre has a booklet detailing walks around Bridgetown. See the Nannup section pp60-61 for walks between Bridgetown and Nannup.

Boyup Brook (Map p119, H9)

Boyup Brook is a small agricultural centre on the Blackwood River, 123km southeast of Bunbury. Its main claim to fame is its reputation as the state capital of country music, and each September there's a weekend festival. The tourist centre (© 08 9765 1444) on the corner of Bridge and Abel Sts can tell you all about it.

In winter/early spring it's possible to canoe down the river from Boyup Brook to the sea. The tourist centre has canoeing guides covering 119km of the river near town, while the caravan park (© 08 9765 1444) hires canoes.

The **Haddleton Nature Reserve**, off Gibbs Rd about 50km northeast of town, is a good spot to see wildflowers and birdlife. Other local attractions include scenic flights, a number of scenic drives in the area, a couple of wineries, and **Glacier Hill**, which is made up of stones that once formed part of the bed of a glacier.

Margaret River Region
(Maps pp118 & 122)

One of the state's major holiday playgrounds, the Margaret River Region is a narrow strip along the coast between Cape Naturaliste in the north and Cape Leeuwin in the south. Its main town is Busselton (pop 11,000), and Augusta, Dunsborough and Margaret River are the largest of the rest. All are holiday resorts whose populations explode over Easter and the summer school holidays.

Mainly noted for its excellent wines, the so-called Cape-to-Cape Coast also offers some fantastic opportunities for outdoor pursuits. The northern coastline is one great surfing break after another. The fishing can be good – particularly when the salmon are running – and there are numerous sheltered reefs ideal for snorkelling. Leeuwin-Naturaliste National Park has some splendid potential for bushwalking, rock climbing and adventure caving.

Wineries

Margaret River's first wine grapes were planted in 1966, yet already the region has earned an international reputation. It produces only about 2% of Australia's wine but accounts for 20% of the premium wines. The secret for this stunning success (apart from astute marketing) is the result of a unique combination of maritime climate and well-drained lateritic soils – the latter particularly favour the cultivation of red varieties. Margaret River already produces some of the country's top chardonnay, semillon, cabernet sauvignon and shiraz. As the vines get older, the reds can only get better.

Today there are around 80 wineries with cellar-door sales, and the competition is intense. Many lure imbibers with up-market eateries and art galleries, while others are more laid-back and personal.

Whichever, you won't find too many crook drops here, but you won't find many bargains either. Hopefully the following small selection will give you some idea what to expect. Don't forget that the wineries are scattered along a 90km-long band. Obviously you'll need to allow more than a day if you'd like to do justice to more than seven or eight of them:

- **Amberley** – Thornton Rd, Yallingup. This winery boasts an attractive setting of vineyards and jarrah forest. It has a good restaurant and produces a range of quality wines.
- **Ashbrook Estate** – Harmans Rd South, Willyabrup. The winery is reached by a narrow dirt road that winds through the forest – but don't let that put you off. While the road and tasting area are basic, the wines (mainly whites) are consistently good and reasonably priced.

- **Cape Mentelle** – Wallcliffe Rd, Margaret River. Another low-key place with a reputation for good, reasonably priced wine – the cab sav, shiraz, chardonnay and semillon are all highly regarded. It's off the cycle path between Margaret River and Prevelly Park.
- **Clairault** – Henry Rd, Willyabrup. The winery, which includes a tranquil alfresco restaurant, has a great setting on the edge of the jarrah forest.
- **Cullen Wines** – Caves Rd, Cowaramup. The region's first vines were planted here. Cullens is a popular place with a relatively informal eatery – the food is delicious, and you can wash it down with some of the region's best reds and whites.
- **Haps Vineyard** – Commonage Rd, Yallingup. Produces some excellent light and fortified wines. There's a good pottery gallery on site.
- **Leeuwin Estate** – Stevens Rd, Margaret River. This was one of the first wineries in the region. As well as a large range of great wines it has an art gallery, and a tasteful restaurant that features expansive views of the nearby jarrah forest and music bowl. Its chardonnay has a truly uplifting effect on jaded palates.
- **Moss Brothers** – Caves Rd, Willyabrup. No art galleries or up-market restaurants to lure imbibers to this place, just good wine.
- **Redgate** – Boodjidup Rd, Margaret River. One of the older wineries in the region, with a good reputation, especially the cabernet sauvignon.
- **Vasse Felix** – Caves Rd, Cowaramup. This is another high-profile winery with great reds and whites. The complex features a restaurant and an art gallery that receives major touring exhibitions.
- **Voyager Estate** – Stevens Rd, Margaret River. One of the larger wineries, with excellent chardonnay, cab merlot and shiraz, a good restaurant and beautiful gardens and lawns. The Cape Dutch architecture and Dutch East India Company (VOC) logo disguise a thoroughly modern operation.
- **Wise Wine** – Eagle Bay Rd, Dunsborough. The main attraction here is an up-market restaurant with sweeping views over Geographe Bay. The cabernet sauvignon is a standout.

Redgate vineyard

Surfing

Almost the entire Margaret River coastline is a happy hunting ground for surfers, with many powerful, mainly left-handed breaks scattered between Dunsborough and **Prevelly Park**, to the west of Margaret River township. The majority of spots south of Cape Naturaliste work best on easterly (i.e. offshore) winds. Getting to some waves requires a bit of effort in the walking or paddling departments, but most are readily accessible off sealed or gravel roads.

The main concentrations of breaks occur around the small coastal settlements of **Yallingup**, **Gracetown** and Prevelly Park, which appear to have grown from surfers' camps in the bush. Each of these places has its own world-class wave: **The Three Bears** north of Yallingup (4WD access only), **North Point** at Gracetown, and **Surfers Point** at Prevelly Park. Considered the state's premier wave, Surfers Point is the venue for two international shortboard competitions (see Surfing pp39-40).

The *Yallingup-Margaret River Surf Map* describes 25 breaks and is a useful reference. It's usually available from the visitor centres in Busselton, Dunsborough and Margaret River.

Surf coast South of Yallingup

South West Corner

63

Board Hire & Surfing Schools

Surfboard Hire (℗ 08 9756 8336) in Dunsborough and Surfside Beach Shack (℗ 08 9755 2036) in Yallingup both hire boards. See p40 for the location of surfing schools.

Cape Naturaliste

Leeuwin-Naturaliste National Park (Maps pp118 F2-J2 & 122 A2-D3)

This 19,700ha park stretches 120km along the coast from Cape Naturaliste to Cape Leeuwin. Its dominant topographic feature is the 200m-high **Leeuwin-Naturaliste Ridge**, which is bordered by spectacular sea cliffs to the west and more gentle slopes on its eastern side. Other notable highlights include granite headlands, sandy beaches, coastal heath (in spring), peppermint-banksia woodlands and dense forests of karri, jarrah and marri.

The ranger's office (℗ 08 9757 2322) is on Bussell Hwy in Margaret River.

What to Do

The park offers major opportunities for trekking, caving and surfing. Other activities include fishing (only in calm conditions, please), snorkelling, mountain-biking, bush camping and abseiling. Guided tours of the lighthouses at Cape Leeuwin and Cape Naturaliste are conducted daily.

A detour off Caves Rd onto Boranup Drive takes you through Boranup Forest, an attractive area of karri regrowth – the original forest was extensively logged between 1882 and 1913 and has recovered nicely. Boranup is 100km from the main karri forest south of Nannup.

The **Wilyabrup Sea Cliffs** north of Gracetown are a major venue for abseiling and climbing, made more pleasurable by great views. Here you find a vertical granite face ranging in height from 32m to next to nothing – you can abseil down, then either climb or walk back to the top. The site includes a 10m-high 'nursery' slope for novice climbers. Groups of five or more must have an accredited leader; abseilers need a permit and climbers are required to register their intentions with the rangers.

Leeuwin-Naturaliste National Park has many fine walks, including the 135km **Cape-to-Cape Track** between Cape Naturaliste and Cape Leeuwin (see boxed text).

Several tracks under 5km wind through the heath that surrounds the historic Cape Naturaliste lighthouse. Highlights include coastal and ocean views and, of course, wildflowers in spring. There are various lookouts, most of which are good for whale-spotting.

The **Yallingup-Smiths Beach** area has a variety of mainly short walks. The 5km Wardanup Trail describes a loop from the Rabbits car park that incorporates the coast, Wardanup Hill and Ngilgi Cave; there are some steep sections along this route. It's about 14km from Yallingup to Cape Naturaliste via the Cape-to-Cape Track.

Further south, at the historic **Ellensbrook Homestead** near Gracetown, a 2km path suitable for wheelchairs features **Meekadarabee Falls** – one of the park's prettiest scenic attractions. The homestead, which dates from 1857, was built by Alfred Bussell, the first European settler in the district.

The park has around 190 known limestone caves, including five **show caves** (Jewel, Lake, Mammoth, Moondyne and Ngilgi) that may be visited on tours. Each show cave has its own appeal (e.g. Jewel Cave is noted for its intricate decorations and Lake Cave for its lake) and you could visit them all without dying of boredom. For information on tour times, contact the CaveWorks Interpretive Centre (℗ 08 9757 7411), off Caves Rd about 16km south of Margaret River. The centre, which opens from 9am to 5pm daily, is a fascinating introduction to the world of caves. There are some great opportunities for adventure caving as well – see the What to Do chapter.

Humpback and southern right whales can be seen from a number of lookouts as they

Rob Boegheim

Cape Leeuwin lighthouse

Rob van Driesum

Boranup Drive

Rob van Driesum

Ellensbrook Homestead

Rob van Driesum

Meekadarabee Falls, a spring-fed waterfall in a grotto, known to Aboriginal people as the "bathing place of the moon"

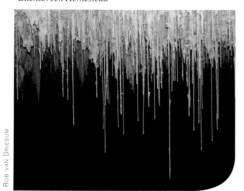

Rob van Driesum

So-called 'straws' in Jewel Cave

Rob van Driesum

The Organ Pipes in Jewel Cave

South West Corner

Walking between the Capes

Walking the 136km **Cape-to-Cape Track** between Cape Naturaliste and Cape Leeuwin, in Leeuwin-Naturaliste National Park, puts you in touch with some of the South West's most spectacular coastal views. The track basically follows the top of a narrow ridge of limestone that sits on granite. It wanders through a diverse range of ecosystems, from stunted heath to majestic karri, with many detours to the coast.

A person of reasonable fitness could comfortably walk the track from end to end in six days. Others may only want to do a day walk, or just experience it in a series of small bites. The latter option is made possible by the numerous access points where public roads either cross or pass close to the track.

The track has been broken into five more-or-less equal sections, each with its own map and notes. Each section has road access to both ends, and at least one designated camping area:

Scenic rock formations at Cosy Corner

- **Cape Naturaliste to Wyadup** (20km) – Route mainly follows a cliff top with stunning views all the way and beach access at Yallingup and Smiths Beach. There's a 1.5km beach walk between these two places, followed by another great view from above Wyadup.

- **Wyadup to Cowaramup Bay** (27km) – The track is confined within a narrow coastal strip for this entire section. Some magnificent scenery as you walk along high, rugged cliff tops.

- **Cowaramup Bay to Redgate Beach** (31km) – Walking conditions are much easier and two inland loops add variety. Highlights include Ellensbrook Homestead, Cape Mentelle and the Boodjidup Brook valley.

- **Redgate Beach to Hamelin Bay** (29km) – Here the park reaches its widest point (6km) and there is plenty of variety in

Canal Rocks, near Yallingup

the scenery and walking experiences. Highlights include magnificent views from the cliff top between Bob's Hollow and Conto's, and the entire 8km section within Boyanup Forest.

- **Hamelin Bay to Cape Leeuwin** (29km) The track features a long beach walk, which can be a slog, and a sense of isolation. Vehicle access is restricted to 4WD, so there aren't many people about. Cosy Corner is a scenic highlight as are the views from high points between here and Hamelin Bay.

For further information, contact the CALM office at 14 Queen St, Busselton (✆ 08 9752 1677) or visit CALM's website (www.naturebase.net).

Several tour operators offer guided walks along the Cape-to-Cape Track, including Adventure In, Inspiration Outdoors, Merribrook and Shaw Horizons. See the beginning of the What to Do chapter for contact details.

The 'frozen waterwheel' at Cape Leeuwin

swim along the Cape-to-Cape Coast during their annual migration. The best places are Cape Naturaliste, **Sugarloaf** (near Cape Naturaliste), North Point (near Gracetown) and Cape Leeuwin, and the busiest times are June and October/November. The *Ocean Giants Lookout Kit* (WATC), with its map showing lookout points along the Cape-to-Cape Coast, is a handy reference for whale watchers.

Busselton jetty

Busselton (Map p118, G4)

This attractive agricultural and tourist centre, 53km southwest of Bunbury, is well protected from the prevailing westerly winds – what is bad news for windsurfers is good for the rest of us! From here it's just 46km to Margaret River, in the heart of the wineries. The Busselton Tourist Bureau (✆ 08 9752 1288, www.down south.com.au) at 38 Peel Terrace has a lot of information on the district's activity-based attractions.

What to See & Do

Stretching 2km into Geographe Bay, Busselton's timber **jetty** has long been a magnet for scuba divers. Here you'll find an amazingly rich variety and abundance of marine life clustered around the jetty's piles. These colourful displays of corals and sponges, along with other life forms such as nudibranchs, molluscs and swarming schools of fish, owe their existence to the warm Leeuwin Current (see p40) and the shelter provided by the jetty. The end result is a spectacle that has to be seen to be believed.

A day trip incorporating a dive on the Busselton jetty and another on the wreck of HMAS *Swan*, near Dunsborough, makes for an unforgettable experience. You can do this with any of the dive centres in Busselton and Dunsborough (see p39).

A more alien spectacle for scuba divers at the jetty is the sight of human faces staring at them from the windows of the new **underwater observatory**. A visit to this 9.5m-diameter concrete structure, at the end of the jetty in eight metres of water, is a must for anyone with even a passing interest in the marine world. Entry to the observatory costs $12.50, and the train ride out from the shore is $7.50 return.

The jetty is popular for **fishing**, with squid, tailor, whiting and herring being common catches; it's also a good crabbing spot. Boats 'n Bikes (✆ 0439 979 360) rents outboard-powered dinghies from the jetty.

Along the coast between Busselton and Bunbury, the attractive **Ludlow Tuart Forest National Park** features the world's largest remaining stand of tuarts. There are no facilities for visitors, but the forest has a fairly open floor – you can park beside the road and go for a walk from there. The park is a critical refuge for several endangered fauna species including Carnaby's black-cockatoo, the chuditch, brush-tailed phascogale and western ring-tailed possum.

Southern Skydivers (✆ 0439 979 897, www.southernskydivers.com.au) offers **tandem skydives** and free-falling courses at the Busselton Airport.

Where to Stay

Busselton's large number of caravan parks attests to its popularity as a resort town:

- Acacia Caravan Park – ✆ 08 9755 4034
- Amblin Caravan Park – ✆ 08 9755 4079, www.amblin-caravanpark.com.au
- Beachlands Holiday Park – ✆ 08 9752 2107, www.beachlands.com
- Busselton Holiday Village – ✆ 08 9752 4499
- Four Seasons Holiday Resort – ✆ 08 9755 4082, www.fourseasonsresort.com.au
- Geographe Bay Holiday Park – ✆ 08 9752 4396
- Kookaburra Caravan Park – ✆ 08 9752 1516, kookpark@compwest.net.au
- Lazy Days Caravan Park – ✆ 08 9752 1780

- Mandalay Holiday Resort & Tourist Park – ✆ 08 9752 1328, www.mandalayresort.com.au
- Sandy Bay Holiday Resort – ✆ 08 9752 2003, www.sandybayresort.com

Dunsborough (Map p118, G3)

On the shores of Geographe Bay 76km from Bunbury, Dunsborough (pop 2500) is the second-largest town in the Margaret River Region. It's an attractive place with easy access to marvellous swimming beaches and the region's wineries and surfing breaks. French place names in the area recall the 1801 visit of Baudin's scientific expedition.

The Dunsborough Tourist Bureau (✆ 08 9755 3299, www.downsouth.com.au) is on Seymour Boulevard.

What to Do

There are **walking tracks** with whale lookouts at nearby Cape Naturaliste (see the section on Leeuwin Naturaliste National Park), and in the 550ha **Meelup Regional Park** between Dunsborough and Cape Naturaliste. The 7km coastal track between the town's northern outskirts and **Eagle Bay** offers terrific scenery, with swimming beaches and whale lookouts en route. Each year, at the time of the February full moon, local naturalists hold a Moon Walk that culminates in a picnic at beautiful **Meelup Beach**. The idea is that you get there in time to watch the moon rise over Geographe Bay. For details, contact Bernie and Carolina Masters on ✆ 08 9727 2474.

Off the coast near Dunsborough is the former naval destroyer **HMAS *Swan***, which was scuttled in 1997 and now forms one of the state's premier dives. The wreck is about 120m

Meelup Beach, a nice place for a swim near Dunsborough

DENIS O'BYRNE

South West Corner

in length and sits upright on a sandy bottom at a depth of 30m – the upper deck is 15m down, where average visibility in summer is 20-25m. A wealth of marine life has already colonised the wreck, which is surrounded by a 500m no-fishing zone.

Dive shops based in Busselton and Dunsborough offer trips that include dives on HMAS *Swan* and the Busselton Jetty.

There's some great snorkelling and diving in the sheltered bays north of Dunsborough, where the diversity of marine life on and around the reefs is (once again) extraordinary. As well, the underwater topography is often spectacular, and the water clarity usually excellent. Not surprisingly, this area is included in a proposed marine park.

There's good sea kayaking here as well – you can launch at Meelup Beach or the boat ramp at the northern end of town. Cape Kayaks (✆ 08 9755 2728, www.capeweb.com.au) and Dekked Out Adventures both do kayaking trips along the Meelup coast.

This area is also excellent for fishing. The eastern end of **Bunker Bay**, on the lee side of Cape Naturaliste, is one of the South West's best salmon spots, but be prepared for a fair hike from the car park. Eagle Bay and Meelup Beach are both good for herring, sand whiting, salmon and flounder.

Wardandi Nyoongar guides provide a fascinating glimpse of their traditional culture at the **Wardan Cultural Centre** (✆ 08 9756 6566, www.wardan.com.au). The centre is on Injidup Springs Rd, 6km south of Yallingup, and opens from 10am to 4pm daily (closed Tuesdays).

Deep-sea fishing charters, whale-watching trips and horse rides are also available locally.

Margaret River (Map p118, J2)

This prosperous, centrally located little township makes an excellent base from which to explore the wineries, surfing spots and other attractions in this area. However, the place simply goes mad during major holiday periods, making it essential to book accommodation many months in advance.

The Margaret River Visitor Centre (✆ 08 9757 2911, www.margaretriver.com) is on Bussell Hwy at the northern end of town. It includes a showroom devoted to local wineries and their products.

Bird enthusiasts will be impressed by **Eagles Heritage** (✆ 08 9757 2960, www.eaglesheritage.com.au), on Boodjidup Rd about five minutes drive southwest from town. This rescue, rehabilitation and breeding centre for birds of prey has a large collection of raptor species set in 12ha of native bush. It provides a unique opportunity to see such birds at close quarters. Flight displays are held daily at 11am and 1.30pm, weather permitting ($7).

There are a number of good birding spots around Margaret River. Birds Australia's leaflet, *Birdwatching Around Margaret River*, gives details.

River Discovery walks ($25) leave from behind the visitor centre at 9.30am daily. Taking two hours, they introduce you to the plants and bush tucker of the area. Contact ✆ 08 9757 1084 (www.bushtuckertours.com) for information and bookings.

A sealed cycling path (9km) links Margaret River township and the surfing centre of Prevelly Park, while a gravel-surfaced rail trail (12km) takes you between Cowaramup and Margaret River. More adventurous options include the 17km Engine Rd Cycle Trail and the 30km Boulter Rd-Boranup Cycle Trail, both through forested areas.

If you haven't brought your own bicycle, you can hire good-quality mountain bikes from Down South Camping (✆ 08 9758 8966) in Margaret River, or take a guided tour with Dirty Detours (✆ 0417 998 816, www.dirty detours.com) through the Boranup Forest.

The visitor centre has a leaflet that details walking and cycling routes around town.

Canoes can be hired in summer at the **Margaret River mouth**. Only the first 2km or so of the river is trafficable, but the scenery is grand and if you throw a line in you might catch a black bream. It's best to go in calm conditions as strong westerlies make getting back to the start point a difficult exercise.

Where to Stay

The Margaret River region has an abundance of B&Bs, motels, farmstays etc. CALM manages three bush campgrounds (Boranup, Conto's and Point Road) in Leeuwin-Naturaliste National Park. Otherwise there are several caravan parks between Yallingup and Augusta. See the Busselton and Augusta sections for more:

- Caves Caravan Park – Yallingup
  (✆ 08 9755 2196,
  park@cavescaravanpark.com)
- Yallingup Beach Holiday Park – Yallingup
  (✆ 08 9755 2164,
  www.yallingupbeach.com.au)
- Canal Rocks Caravan Park – Smiths Beach
  (✆ 08 9755 2116, www.canalrocks.com.au)
- Taunton Farm Holiday Park – Cowaramup
  (✆ 08 9755 5334,
  www.tauntonfarm.com.au)
- Gracetown Caravan Park – Gracetown
  (✆ 08 9755 5301)
- Prevelly Park Beach Resort –
  Margaret River (✆ 08 9757 2374)
- Riverview Caravan Park – Margaret River
  (✆ 08 9757 2270,
  www.riverviewcabin.com)

Augusta (Map p122, C3)

An attractive little town at the southern end of the Cape-to-Cape Coast, Augusta is handily situated near several regional draws. These include the main group of show caves, Cape Leeuwin, the southern terminus of the Cape-to-Cape Track, and Hardy Inlet.

The Augusta Visitor Centre (✆ 08 9758 0166, www.margaretriver.com) is on the corner of Bussell Hwy and Ellis St.

Augusta is a major whale-watching centre, with humpbacks and southern rights often swimming together in the sheltered waters of Flinders Bay. In 1986 it made world headlines when a mass stranding of 114 false killer whales took place on the town beach.

After working heroically for 60 hours, a small army of volunteers was able to return 96 of them to the sea.

Anglers will be rapt in the variety of fishing venues near town. Hardy Inlet is good for a range of species including black bream, King George whiting and flathead, but you really need a boat. Black bream can be caught all the way up the Blackwood River to Alexandra Bridge.

There's good scuba diving in Hamelin Bay, which has an underwater wreck trail. Closer to town, windsurfing is popular at the mouth of the inlet.

Where to Stay

There is quite a bit of accommodation in and around Augusta, including several budget places:

- Alexandra Bridge Campground –
  ✆ 08 9758 2244
- Baywatch Manor Resort – ✆ 9758 1290,
  www.baywatchmanor.com.au
- Doonbanks Chalets & Caravan Park –
  ✆ 08 9758 1517,
  www.netserve.net.au/doonbank/
- Flinders Bay Caravan Park –
  ✆ 08 9758 1380
- Hamelin Bay Caravan Park – Hamelin Bay
  (✆ 08 9758 5540,
  www.augusta-resorts.com.au)
- Molloy Caravan Park – ✆ 08 9758 4515,
  molloy@augusta-resorts.com.au
- Turner Caravan Park – ✆ 08 9758 1517,
  turnerpark@amrsc.wa.gov.au
- Westbay Retreat Caravan Park –
  ✆ 08 9758 1572 ∎

Glorious Hamelin Bay

Chapter Six

Southern Forests

The Southern Forests include the main concentration of karri, which occurs in a belt running southwards from Nannup through Manjimup and Pemberton to the Frankland River. Here also are forests of jarrah and tingle mixed with marri and yarri (blackbutt). Most of the remaining 190,000ha of karri forest is on public land and features many opportunities for memorable encounters of the tree kind. These include the fire lookout trees near Manjimup and Pemberton, the Great Forest Trees Drive near Northcliffe, and the Tree Top Walk near Nornalup.

The region also has a stunning coastline, with long surf beaches separated by rugged cliffs all the way from Black Point in the west to William Bay in the east. Almost the entire coast is within national parks, and there are many great opportunities for fishing (sea, river and estuarine environments) and four-wheel driving.

Other attractions for energetic visitors include the Bibbulmun Track, which wanders through the forests from One Tree Bridge near Manjimup to Mandalay Beach, past which it mainly hugs the coast. Several rivers have good potential for canoeing, and there are a number of bush campgrounds scattered through the area.

The southern forests are accessible off either the South West Hwy (national route 1) or the Vasse Hwy (state route 10).

Manjimup (Map p123 C8)

On the edge of the big timber country 300km from Perth, Manjimup (pop 4500) is by far the largest town in the Southern Forests, and is the commercial centre for a thriving forestry, horticultural and agricultural hinterland. It's an emerging wine district, with several wineries open for tastings. For more energetic pursuits, there are some good walks in the surrounding forest.

Information

The Manjimup Visitor Centre (✆ 08 9771 1831, 1800 023 388) is on Johnston Cres, and CALM's regional office (✆ 08 9771 7988) is on Brain St.

Things to See & Do

Manjimup has several cellar doors, the best known being the **Chestnut Grove Winery**, 8km from town off Perup Rd. It produces award-winning wines *and* olive oil. Others worth visiting are **Fontys Pool Wines** (8km out on 7 Day Rd) and **Peos Estate** (11km out on Graphite Rd).

About 3km out on Perup Rd, an ancient **king jarrah** measuring 2m across at the girth rises straight up towards the sky, the great column of its trunk surmounted by a tangle of branches. It's not the world's largest tree by any means, but you come away thinking what a magical place the original jarrah forests must have been.

The **Perup Forest Ecology Centre** 50km east of Manjimup lies within the 52,000ha Perup Nature Reserve. This is a good spot to see several native mammal species including ring-tail possums, brush-tail possums, woylies, phascogales and tammar wallabies. Guided tours are currently available only to large groups (20 or more) but this may change when a caretaker is appointed. Meanwhile, self-guided nocturnal tours cost $10 per person including bunkhouse accommodation – bring your own bedding. Bookings should be made at CALM's Manjimup office.

On the South Western Hwy 8km south of town, the **Diamond Tree** is one of the original fire lookout karri trees (see the boxed text p73).

One Tree Bridge, in mature and regrowth karri forest on Graphite Drive about 19km west of town, was based on a single huge log felled across the Donnelly River in 1904. It's now rotting away on dry ground on the northern side of the road – to get there, follow the walkway under the 'new' bridge. A 2km return walk leads from the bridge to four impressive karris called the **Four Aces**. These towering giants, which appear to have been planted in a row, are estimated to be 250 years old. You can walk from here to Willow Springs, 32km north, by following the Bibbulmun Track (see p25). Trout and marron can be caught in the river.

At Tone River Settlement, off Muirs Hwy to the east of Manjimup, the 14km **Maxwell Track** winds through jarrah and flooded gum along the Tone River and ends at Chindilup Pool. The visitor centre has a map.

See the section on Nannup (pp60-61) for the location of forest walks in the area between Manjimup, Nannup and Bridgetown.

Pemberton (Map p123, D7-D8)

Located in farmland and karri forest 33km southwest of Manjimup, the picturesque little timber town of Pemberton is within easy striking distance of several regional highlights. These include two fire lookout trees, and the old-growth karri forests of Beedelup and Warren national parks. Also near town are several wineries, and good trout fishing in the Warren River and its tributaries.

Information

The Pemberton Visitor Centre (℡ 08 9776 1133, 1800 671 133, www.pembertontourist.com.au) is on Brockman St (the main thoroughfare). The complex includes a forest interpretive centre.

CALM's Donnelly district office (℡ 08 9776 1207) is on the corner of Kennedy and Robinson Sts. Rangers based here can answer your questions on Beedelup, D'Entrecasteaux, Gloucester and Warren national parks, and Big Brook State Forest.

What to See & Do

The first commercial **winery** in the Pemberton area was established in 1983, and already local vignerons have earned a fine reputation for their cool-climate wines. At last count 13 wineries – mostly small, family-owned boutiques – were offering cellar-door sales, and more are opening all the time. Tall Timber Adventure Treks does a guided tour of up to six cellar doors.

Pemberton's single major attraction would have to be the fire lookout tower on top of the **Gloucester Tree**, 3km east of town in the 874ha **Gloucester National Park**. It offers a challenging climb that ends in a superb view over the surrounding forest and farmland. In busy times there's often a queue of people waiting to climb, so it pays to get there early. On the other hand, late afternoon on a sunny day brings the best light conditions for photographing the action.

The Pemberton area has a number of mostly short (less than 2km) forest walks and these are detailed in the booklet *Pemberton Bushwalks*, available from the visitor centre. Longer ones include the Bibbulmun Track, which passes the Gloucester Tree en route between Pemberton and Beedelup Falls, in Beedelup National Park. Also recommended is the 6km linear track that links the Gloucester Tree with the **Cascades**, a picturesque feature on Lefroy Brook.

For a different way to experience the forest, take a ride in a steam-powered train or diesel tram from the old Pemberton train station. Trams leave daily at 10.45am and 2pm, and take you south to the Warren River bridge and back – the return journey takes about two hours including a stop at the Cascades. Because of fire restrictions, the steam **train** only operates from Easter to early November. For inquiries and bookings, contact The Pemberton Tramway Co (℡ 08 9776 1322, www.pemtram.com.au).

Six km north of Pemberton, the **Big Brook State Forest** is a beautiful area of karri regrowth from the 1920s, when the original forest was clear-felled. **Big Brook Dam** is a great spot for picnics, walks, swimming and

The Cascades along Lefroy Brook

Forest Lookouts

A plume of black smoke rising from the trees in the tinder-dry conditions of summer strikes fear into the heart of all forest managers. The immediate challenge is to extinguish the flames before they get out of control. To have any hope of doing this in an area as large as the Southern Forest requires a method of fixing the smoke's location so that fire-fighting crews can be rushed to the spot.

There were no spotter planes when forestry operations expanded into karri country. A network of fire lookouts built on high ground had worked well in the jarrah forest, but there were few hills high enough to see over the karris. This problem was solved by building fire lookouts in the tallest trees.

The task of constructing a fire lookout tree was an adventure in itself. First the chosen tree had to be climbed in order to check its suitability, then a spiral ladder was constructed around the trunk – each rung was hammered into the tree after a hole had been drilled by a person sitting on the rung below. The top of the tree was then lopped using an axe, and the lookout constructed.

Thirteen fire lookouts, most of them perched in tall karris, were constructed in the forest. The Diamond Tree near Manjimup and the Bicentennial and Gloucester trees, both near Pemberton, are open to the public and have become major tourist attractions. The tallest is the Bicentennial Tree at a little over 60m.

The Bicentennial Tree – climbing it is not for the faint-hearted

ROB VAN DRIESUM

fishing (stocked with rainbow trout). The **Big Brook Arboretum** is also here, a 50-year-old garden of interstate and overseas trees planted to see how they would grow in karri country.

The **Karri Forest Explorer** is an 86km-long, self-guided driving tour that starts in Pemberton and describes a loop around the town, taking in places like Beedelup and Warren national parks. En route there are signs to guide you and 'radio stops' to describe the various highlights. Pick up a leaflet from the visitor centre.

Pemberton Hiking & Trekking and Tall Timber Adventure Treks offer a range of activity-based tours in this area.

Where to Stay

There are numerous B&Bs, farmstays and the like in and around Pemberton. CALM has bush campgrounds in Warren River, otherwise try the following budget places:

- Pemberton Backpackers – ✆ 08 9776 1105
- Pemberton Caravan Park – ✆ 08 9776 1300, www.pembertonpark.com.au
- Pimelea Chalets YHA – ✆ 08 9776 1153

Southern Forests

Warren National Park
(Map p123, D7-E7)

This magnificent park, 10km southwest of Pemberton, covers 3000ha of old-growth karri. There are many impressive individuals in this towering forest of pale-barked giants, including the **Dave Evans Bicentennial Tree** and its fire lookout. The lookout was built in 1988 as part of Australia's Bicentennial celebrations, hence the name – Dave Evans was a local politician and past Minister of Forests. As the queues tend to be shorter here than at the Gloucester Tree, it might be worth heading out to climb this one instead.

Also worth mentioning is the **Heartbreak Trail**, a minor dirt road that forms a loop off Old Vasse Rd – the main route through the forest. The trail descends steeply to the scenic **Warren River**, where there are several attractive bush campgrounds by the water. The complete circuit is about 12km and would make a good mountain-biking route. Don't assume that it'll be an easy ride, though, as there are plenty of testing ascents to make up for the descents.

The suspension bridge across the gorge at Beedelup Falls

Beedelup National Park
(Map p123, D7)

This 1590ha park is on the Vasse Hwy 15km west of Pemberton. Here you'll find beautiful old-growth karri/marri/jarrah forest as well as **Beedelup Falls**. Actually a series of cascades that plunge down a steep, 100m-high granite slope, the falls are one of the area's main scenic attractions – it's nice to relax and listen to the water as it roars (or gurgles, depending on the season) over the rocks. The access path is suitable for wheelchairs.

Northcliffe (Map p123, F8)

The little timber town of Northcliffe, 30km south of Pemberton and just outside the vast D'Entrecasteaux National Park, is an out-of-the way place with some worthwhile attractions for outdoors lovers. Among other things you can go surfing and surf fishing at nearby Windy Harbour, go mountain biking on state-championship tracks, and do any number of forest walks.

There's a Pioneer Museum next to the Northcliffe Visitor Centre (℡ 08 9776 7203, www.northcliffe.org.au) on Wheatley Coast Rd.

Beedelup Falls

Southern Forests

The Northcliffe visitor centre

What to Do

Northcliffe prides itself on being a mountain-biking centre and each year over the March long weekend it hosts the **Karri Cup**, one of the state's premier events for mountain bikers. The venue is the forest tracks around town, and the visitor centre has maps if you want to check them at other times. Hire bikes are available locally.

On the edge of town, the **Northcliffe Forest Park** boasts a variety of forest types including old-growth karri, marri and mixed marri/jarrah. There are also riverine and coastal wetland communities. The park has several good, mainly short walks, including a 400m wheelchair-friendly path through a patch of virgin karri. The longest track here is the 3.5km **Marri Meander**, a moderately difficult loop walk through mature karri before entering the very different world of a marri forest.

Heading eastwards out of town on Middleton Rd you come to the **Jane Forest Trail**, an 11km loop walk through old-growth karri, marri and jarrah. The visitor centre has a leaflet that describes this enjoyable trek.

Continue east on Middleton Rd to the turn-off to the 616ha **Boorara Conservation Park**. There are mountain-bike trails here as well as mixed jarrah/karri/marri forest. In winter or spring you can view picturesque **Lane Poole Falls**, accessible by a 5km walk from the Boorara Tree picnic area – the falls are dry during summer/autumn.

Where to Stay

If Windy Harbour and Pemberton are full, you can usually find somewhere to stay at one of the following places in Northcliffe:

- Northcliffe Caravan Park – ℂ 08 9776 7295
- Northcliffe Hotel – ℂ 08 9776 7089
- Bibbulmun Break Motel – ℂ 08 9776 6060

D'Entrecasteaux National Park
(Maps pp122 D5-E6 & 123 E7-H10)

This magnificent, 116,700ha park stretches for 130km along the coast from Black Point in the west to Long Point near Walpole in the east, and extends inland for up to 20km. It features a diversity of landforms including long white beaches, rugged cliffs, shifting dunes, rivers, swamps and lakes, as well as karri and jarrah forests and coastal heath. The activities on offer here include bush camping, beach and rock fishing, surfing and four-wheel driving. However, most of the park is remote and difficult to get to, and visitors to these areas should be well prepared and self-sufficient in everything. With the exception of the access roads to Windy Harbour (a tiny holiday-ville near Point D'Entrecasteaux), Salmon Beach and Mandalay Beach, all routes leading to the coast are strictly 4WD only.

Information

Rangers based at Walpole manage the park's eastern end. Contact the CALM office in Pemberton for information on the area west of Broke Inlet.

What to See & Do – 2WD

The walk to the top of **Mt Chudalup** (187m) provides a sweeping view over seasonal wetlands and tree islands to the sea. Allow an hour for the return walk, which includes a steep forest path and bare granite slopes – footwear that gives a good grip on slippery surfaces is recommended. Mt Chudalup is beside Windy Harbour Rd just inside the park boundary.

Just west of Windy Harbour, **Point D'Entrecasteaux** features rugged limestone cliffs and extensive views of the coast and islands. Not surprisingly, it's a prime spot for watching whales. A walking track, part of which is designed to be wheelchair-friendly, is being constructed from Windy Harbour to Salmon Beach via Point D'Entrecasteaux. There's 2WD access to **Salmon Beach**, which is popular with fishers and surfers – swimming is not recommended, though.

At the park's eastern end, **Broke Inlet** on the Shannon River is a large, shallow estuary connected to the sea by a seasonal channel. It's the only one of the South West's larger estuaries not to be significantly altered by developments either in its catchment or along its shores. The northern shore is accessible to conventional

Southern Forests

ROB BOEGHEIM

Salmon Beach

To access the long, sweeping **Yeagarup Beach,** you turn off Vasse Hwy onto Ritter Rd. The fun begins past **Yeagarup Lake**, where you're faced with crossing the white, desert-like wastes of the **Yeagarup Dunes**. This exercise is difficult at the best of times and shouldn't be tackled by novices unless accompanied by an expert. Stay between the markers, please.

Next is the **Warren Beach Track**, the most difficult route of all. This track, which can be reached off either Vasse Hwy or Richardson Rd from Northcliffe, features a tough dune crossing that requires a high level of off-road driving skill. Once you get over that obstacle it's relatively easy going to **Warren Beach**, the access point being about 3km south of the Warren River mouth. The mouth is a great surf-fishing spot yielding herring, skippy, tarwhine, salmon, mulloway and tailor.

Depending on the condition of the Warren and Meerup river mouths, you can drive right along the beach from **Donnelly Rocks** (near the Donnelly River mouth) to **Malimup Rocks**, a distance of about 36km. Camping is permitted on the beach and behind the foredune, and there are plenty of good fishing spots along the way.

Turning off Windy Harbour Rd, the **Summertime Track** ends at **Malimup Beach**. There is vehicle access onto the beach, but rocks prevent travel to the south. The track crosses seasonal swampland and is impassable for much of the year – hence the name.

The tracks to **Gardner Beach, Coodamurrup Beach** and **Fish Creek** all turn off Chesapeake Rd, which can be reached off either the South Western Hwy or Windy Harbour Rd. These are sandy but straightforward, though the Fish Creek Track is rough in parts. You can reach the mouth of the **Gardner River** by driving along the beach from either Fish Creek or Windy Harbour, but the river mouth itself is impassable. The Gardner is canoeable for several km upstream from its mouth. Once again, you can camp on the beach or behind the foredune.

To the east of Mandalay Beach, the **Long Point Track** forms the border between the D'Entrecasteaux and Walpole-Nornalup national parks. **Long Point** itself features spectacular granite headlands. Rock fishers can make some good catches here, provided a king wave doesn't get them first! The same can be

vehicles via Broke Inlet Rd off the South Western Hwy. Access to the mouth is 4WD only via Fishermans Rd off Mandalay Beach Rd. This route is closed from June to November.

Gutters along **Mandalay Beach**, 19km west of Walpole, yield salmon, herring, tailor, mulloway and sand whiting, and if the fish aren't biting you can at least enjoy the superb coastal scenery. Mandalay Beach is a vehicle-access point for the Bibbulmun Track. The name recalls the Norwegian barque *Mandalay*, which was wrecked on the beach here in 1911.

What to See & Do – 4WD

To explore this park in any depth you need a 4WD vehicle with good ground clearance and low-range gearing. You will also need a tyre-pressure gauge and a compressor, as all the tracks mentioned here include deep, soft sand. Most of the park's 4WD routes lead to fishing and bush-camping spots.

Starting at the park's western end, **Black Point** features spectacular sea cliffs consisting of tall columns of basalt. This popular fishing and surfing spot can be reached off either Black Point Rd (closed by flooding from May until after Christmas) or Milyeannup Coast Rd. Another route is the Wapet Track, which is off Scott Rd via **Lake Jasper**. One of the state's largest natural bodies of freshwater, it's a popular marroning and windsurfing spot.

Getting to the mouth of the Donnelly River is a little different. First, turn off the Vasse Hwy onto Boat Landing Rd and follow it to where it stops at a picnic area by the river. From here you take to the water for the final 14km or so to the river mouth, where there's excellent beach and inlet fishing.

Southern Forests

said for **Cliffy Head**, a 4WD destination just to the west of Mandalay Beach. It offers outstanding views along the coast towards Windy Harbour.

Where to Stay

CALM provides bush campgrounds at Black Point, Lake Jasper, Carey Brook (on Boat Landing Rd), Moore's Hut (on the track to Coodamurrup Beach) and Crystal Springs (at the Mandalay Beach turn-off on the South Western Hwy).

Alternatively, try the Windy Harbour Campground (✆ 08 9776 8398).

Shannon National Park
(Map p123, E9-E10)

On the South Western Hwy 50km southeast of Manjimup, this 53,500ha park incorporates the entire catchment of the Shannon River – great news for the health of Broke Inlet. Apart from the river, the main features of this area include old-growth karri forest, seasonal wetlands, heaths and granite domes. The forests here were largely left alone until the late 1940s, when the Shannon timber mill and associated township were established. The mill was closed 20 years later and the buildings dismantled, but exotic trees such as pines and fruit trees show where the town was located. This area is now the Shannon Campsite, a lovely camping spot.

The 48km **Great Forest Trees Drive**, which describes a loop from the campground, is a popular scenic route that takes in various highlights such as picnic spots, the Snake Gully Lookout and Big Tree Grove. There are a number of 'radio stops' along the way where FM broadcasts tell you about various aspects of the forest.

Walking tracks provide access from the camping area to **Shannon Dam** and **Mokare's Rock**. The former supplied water to the Shannon Mill, while Mokare was a Nyoongar interpreter and guide to the early military commanders at Albany. Climb the rock for great views over the Shannon Basin. Another walk, the 8km **Great Forest Trees Trail**, connects the two northern arms of the scenic drive.

Shannon National Park is managed from CALM's Walpole office.

Magnificent karri at Snake Gully lookout

Mt Frankland National Park
(Map p123, F11-G12)

Along with Shannon National Park, this 30,800ha park contains the largest remaining stands of virgin karri forest. Most of the relatively few visitors come to climb Mt Frankland, a large granite dome reaching 411m above sea level. The summit, which is topped by a fire lookout, offers a stunning view over a vast wilderness of trees dotted with a few islands of farmland – on a clear day you can see Bluff Knoll, 145km to the east in the Stirling Range. The dome rises 150m above its base and makes a good abseiling and climbing venue. It takes about an hour for the return walk to the top, and about 30 minutes to do the walk around the base.

Mt Frankland is about 27km north of Walpole via North Walpole Rd and Frankland Rd. The road ends at a small bush-camping area a short walk from the mount.

Southern Forests

77

The seemingly endless view from Mt Frankland

ROB VAN DRIESUM

Walpole (Map p123, H11)

On the South Coast Hwy 118km southeast of Manjimup, the pretty little township of Walpole and its even smaller neighbour Nornalup are surrounded by the forests of the 18,000ha Walpole-Nornalup National Park. Walpole just about begs you to linger awhile to check the diverse attractions near town. These include the famous Tree Top Walk, Nornalup Inlet (where the Deep and Frankland rivers meet the sea), and spectacular coastal scenery at places like Mandalay Beach, Long Point and Conspicuous Cliff. Walking, canoeing and fishing are popular activities.

Information

The Walpole-Nornalup Visitor Centre (© 08 9840 1111, www.southernforests.com .au) is on the South Western Highway.

CALM's district office (© 08 9840 1207) on the South Western Hwy at the western end of town manages Shannon, Frankland, Walpole-Nornalup and William Bay national parks and the eastern end of D'Entrecasteaux National Park.

What to See & Do

The Walpole area has plenty of good things to do, but the **Tree Top Walk** in the aptly named **Valley of the Giants** is by far the most popular destination for visitors. Here, 23km east of town near Nornalup, a 600m-long steel walkway that rises to 40m above the valley floor provides the unique experience of walking through the forest canopy. The ramps slope gently and are suitable for wheelchairs. Entry costs $6 and the opening hours are 9am to 4.15pm daily (8am to 5.15pm in the summer school holidays).

At ground level adjacent to the Tree Top Walk, a boardwalk takes you through a grove of huge red tingles known as the **Ancient Empire**. These magnificent specimens are up to 16m in circumference and 60m in height.

For something less adventurous, the 3km Coalmine Beach Heritage Trail is a nice, part-bush, part-urban walk from the Walpole Visitor Centre to **Coalmine Beach**, a popular swimming and windsurfing spot on **Nornalup Inlet**. The trail forms part of the Bibbulmun Track.

Another good walk on the Bibbulmun Track takes you between the vehicle access points at **Conspicuous Cliff** and **Peaceful Bay,** a distance of about 13km. There are stunning coastal views almost the whole way. Conspicuous Cliff is great for surfing and surf fishing, while Peaceful Bay offers safe swimming and snorkelling behind a granite reef. A network of sandy 4WD tracks links fishing spots between these two places.

Heading east from Walpole, there's 4WD access onto the beaches at **Bellenger Beach**, **Rame Head** and Peaceful Bay. Bellenger Beach, which is soft and sloping, isn't recommended for beginners. The vehicle access point is about

Tree Top Walk in the Valley of the Giants

Buttressed red tingle near Hilltop Lookout

Tree Top Walk in the Valley of the Giants

halfway along and you can drive to both ends of the beach from here. Talk to the rangers in Walpole before attempting any of the 4WD tracks in this area.

On Hilltop Rd about 5km east of Walpole, **Hilltop Lookout** gives a fine view over the Frankland River and Nornalup Inlet. Continue another 3km to a car park, where an 800m walking track takes you on a circuit past a giant **red tingle** with a girth of 24m – a truly magnificent specimen. Continue along Hilltop Rd and you eventually come to **Circular Pool** on the Frankland. A raging torrent in winter, it's

Southern Forests

Greens Pool, a sheltered family beach in William Bay NP

a restful picnic and swimming spot in summer. Virtually the entire drive from Walpole to Circular Pool is on narrow, unsealed, one-way roads through dense karri and tingle forest.

Another enjoyable scenic drive, this one mainly sealed, takes you north from town via North Walpole Rd to Mt Frankland, then west on Beardmore Rd to picturesque **Fernhook Falls** on the Deep River. Beardmore Rd continues west to the South Western Hwy, where you return to Walpole via the lookout on **Mt Pingerup**. The total distance of this tour is about 85km.

In winter and early spring you can launch your canoe or kayak at Fernhook Falls and paddle down to the South Western Hwy, although most people only go as far as Centre Rd (a distance of about 24km). You can also paddle down the Frankland from Bridge Rd to the inlet.

The lower Frankland offers an enjoyable canoeing experience in summer as well – you launch at the Nornalup Bridge and paddle upstream to the tidal limit at **Monastery Landing**, then head back down to the inlet before returning to the bridge. This makes for a very pleasant excursion of around 16km. Incidentally, there was never a house of God at Monastery Landing; apparently whoever named it thought that there was something religious about the reflections and atmosphere.

Canoes can be hired for $60 per day from Nornalup Riverside Chalets (© 08 9840 1107).

Accessible only by 4WD vehicle, **Boat Harbour** is a sheltered bay offering dramatic coastal scenery, camping, fishing and swim-ming. The turn-off is on the South Coast Hwy 41km east of Walpole.

There are more spectacular views further east in the 1900ha **William Bay National Park,** which also features mobile dunes, karri forest and extensive coastal heathlands. Granite reefs have created safe swimming areas at Madfish Bay and beautiful Greens Pool. Madfish Island – you can wade across at low tide – has sea-bird rookeries and many poisonous snakes. Accessible by the Bibbulmun Track, Tower Hill presents a striking landscape of granite outcrops and karri trees.

Where to Stay

In this general area you'll find CALM campgrounds at Crystal Springs (12km west), Fernhook Falls (39km northwest) and Mt Frankland (27km north), and a shire campground at Parry Beach (49km east). There are also these budget places:

- Coalmine Beach Holiday & Caravan Park –
  © 1800 670 026,
  www.coalminebeach. com.au
- Peaceful Bay Caravan Park –
  © 08 9840 8060,
  peaceful@omninet.net.au
- Rest Point Holiday Village –
  © 08 9840 1032,
  restpoint@westnet.com.au
- Tingle All Over – © 08 9840 1041
- Valley of the Giants Ecopark –
  © 08 9840 1313,
  www.valleyofthegiantsecopark.biz
- Walpole Backpackers – © 08 9840 1244,
  www.walpolebackpackers.com ∎

The South Coast stretches from Denmark in the west to beyond Esperance in the east and extends up to 100km inland. It includes the regional centres of Albany and Esperance, both of which are on the South Coast Hwy (national route 1).

Looking at the coast west of Albany you'll wonder how the views could possibly get any better, only to find that the further east you go the more awesome they become. In stark contrast to the Southern Forests, most of the original vegetation in inland areas has been cleared for agriculture. Here, a few conservation reserves are islands of biodiversity in a sea of wheat paddocks.

Albany Region

The Albany Region includes the Stirling Range, Porongurup and Fitzgerald River national parks, all of which are among WA's most spectacular conservation areas in terms of native flora and/or scenery. Two Peoples Bay is famous for its endangered birds and mammals, including two species that were 'rediscovered' here after being presumed extinct.

Outdoors lovers will find plenty to keep themselves occupied in the Albany Region. There are several good spots for hang-gliding, abseiling, rock climbing and surfing, while bushwalking, scuba diving, fishing and whale-watching are all popular. West Cape Howe National Park only covers 3500ha, but it provides opportunities for almost all these activities. As well, there's a growing wine industry, with numerous cellar doors mainly centred on Denmark, Mt Barker and Porongurup.

Wineries

The first vineyard in what is now called the Great Southern Wine Region was only established in 1967, but already the area has gained a fine reputation for its cool-climate riesling and, to a lesser extent, chardonnay and shiraz. Today, more than 30 cellar doors are scattered over an area of about 1000 sq km stretching from north of Mt Barker and the Stirling Range to Albany and Denmark. Most are small, family-owned labels. The tasting areas are generally low-key, and you can invariably enjoy a friendly chat while indulging your taste buds. You'll find plenty of bargains, too. The following is just a tiny sample:

- **Fox River Wines** – Albany Hwy, Mt Barker. Some visitors will take one look at the 'modernistic' design of this winery and decide to keep on driving. That would be a mistake, as its offerings are worth stopping for.
- **Jingalla Wines** – Bolganup Rd, Porongurup. This friendly little place has a pleasant setting among gardens and native trees located on the entrance road into the Porongurup National Park. It was the first winery in the Porongurup district, and is best known for its riesling, shiraz and liqueur muscat.
- **Plantagenet Wines** – Albany Hwy, Mt Barker. The region's first commercial winery has won many awards, particularly for its riesling, shiraz and cabernet sauvignon. The cosy tasting area (there's a fire in winter) is in a converted apple-packing shed close to the centre of town.
- **The Lily** – Chester Pass Rd, Stirling Range. This isolated winery produces a good drop but it is better known for its replica Dutch windmill – an amazing sight in the Australian countryside – and excellent meals. You'll find it about 12km north of the Stirling Range National Park.
- **Matilda's Estate** – Hamilton Rd, Denmark. Unwooded chardonnay and pinot noir are strong points of this pleasantly situated winery. There's a café-style restaurant and regular live-music performances in summer.
- **West Cape Howe Wines** – South Coast Hwy, Denmark. Standouts here are cabernet sauvignon and unwooded chardonnay.

Farm west of Denmark

Denmark (Map p124, H4)

On the Denmark River 51km west of Albany, this attractive town lies just outside the eastern end of the main belt of karri forest. It's a busy tourism and agricultural centre with a growing wine industry. The Denmark Tourist Bureau (✆ 08 9848 2055, touristb@denmarkwa .net.au) is at 60 Strickland St in the town centre.

What to See & Do

Denmark is handy to a number of attractions such as wineries, the Tree Top Walk, William Bay and West Cape Howe. The springtime wildflowers and coastal scenery are stunning.

Wilson Inlet, at the Denmark River mouth just south of town, is good for windsurfing and fishing – a range of species including pink snapper, flathead, King George whiting, black bream and blue manna crabs are caught here.

Ocean Beach, 10km south at the inlet's mouth, is famous for its surf fishing and has one of the south coast's most powerful surfing breaks. You can go swimming here in summer, but only between the flags. Surfing lessons are available at Ocean Beach with South Coast Surfing (✆ 08 9840 9041, 0415 839 313). **Lights Beach**, on the eastern edge of William Bay National Park, is another popular fishing and surfing spot.

The brochure, *Trails of Denmark*, describes 10 walks from one to 12km. These include the 4.5km track up to the summit of

Mt Lindesay, where you get great views, and a stroll (or cycle) along the old Albany-Nornalup railway alignment.

The Lazy R Pony Stud (✆ 08 9840 9281) on Happy Valley Rd to the west of town can arrange half-day horse rides for competent riders.

Where to Stay

Budget places in Demark include:

- Blue Wren Travellers Rest – ✆ 08 9848 3300
- Karri Mia Resort – ✆ 08 9848 2233, www.karrimia.com.au (has drive-through caravan bays)
- Ocean Beach Caravan Park – ✆ 08 9848 1105
- Riverbend Chalets & Caravan Park – ✆ 08 9848 1107, riverbend@omninet.net.au
- Rivermouth Caravan Park – ✆ 08 9848 1262

Ocean Beach near Denmark

Albany (Maps pp124 H6 & 125 H7)

Albany (pop 29,000), beside scenic King George Sound 407km from Perth, is the South West's second-largest regional centre after Mandurah. Established in 1826, it was WA's first European settlement, and relics of those early years may still be seen around town. Albany is a busy, prosperous place with an economy based on agriculture, forestry and tourism. With all the outdoor attractions in the area it's an excellent place for an activities-based holiday.

Information

The Albany Visitor Centre (℡ 08 9841 1088, 1800 644 088, www.albanytourist.com.au) is in the old railway station on Proudlove Parade, on the southern side of the city centre. CALM's office (℡ 08 9842 4500) at 120 Albany Hwy is a mine of information on the parks of this region.

What to See & Do

Albany is a major whale-watching centre and was once home to a thriving industry based on the hunting and processing of humpback whales. Today, the old Cheynes Beach whaling station has been converted into the fascinating **Whale World Museum** (℡ 08 9844 4021, www.whaleworld.org). One of the region's 'must sees', it's on Frenchman Bay about 21km from Albany. The museum opens daily from 9am to 5pm and entry costs $15, including a 45-minute guided tour. Allow at least two hours for a good look.

There are many beautiful beaches around Albany. In the right conditions you'll find good surfing breaks at Middleton's, Nanarup, Sand Patch and Mutton Bird. Middleton's, about 5km east of the CBD, is also a popular swimming spot.

The main attractions for scuba divers are the destroyer HMAS *Perth* and the whale-chaser *Cheynes III*, both of which were scuttled to form dive wrecks, and the rich marine fauna and underwater topography found on numerous limestone and granite reefs in surrounding waters. There are three local dive shops and you'll find their details on p39.

Not surprisingly, the coast has many good fishing spots and 29 of them are pinpointed on a map produced by Albany Rocks & Tackle (℡ 08 9841 1231), on Stirling Terrace. If you want to go fishing on a remote beach, but have neither tackle nor 4WD vehicle, contact Do-A-Tour (℡ 08 9844 3154, doatour@iprimus.com.au). Their half/full day trips cost $60/95. Otherwise head out to sea with one of the local charter boats (see p36).

The Albany Reef Explorer (℡ 0418 950 361, www.albanyreefexplorer.com.au) is a semi-submersible vessel that does underwater viewing cruises in King George Sound. Other tours available locally include scenic flights and whale-watching trips

The **Mt Martin Regional Botanic Park,** 7km east northeast of town, is described as being "representative of the area's endemic flora". There are 11km of walking tracks with some steep, rough sections, but the stunning coastal views and spring wildflowers make it all worthwhile. The park is accessed from the Ledge Point Beach car park. For information, contact the City of Albany rangers on ℡ 08 9841 0333.

Where to Stay

Albany has a lot of accommodation including these budget places:

- Albany Backpackers – ℡ 08 9841 8848
- Bayview YHA – ℡ 08 9842 3388, albany@hawa.com.au
- Albany Happy Days Caravan Park – ℡ 08 9844 3267, happyday@omninet.net.au
- Albany Tourist Village – ℡ 08 9841 3752, atourvil@omninet.net.au
- Emu Beach Holiday Park – ℡ 08 9844 1147, 1800 984 411, www.emubeach.com
- Frenchman Bay Caravan Park – ℡ 08 9844 4015
- Kalgan River Chalets & Caravan Park – ℡ 08 9844 7937, www.wn.com.au/cb
- Middleton Beach Holiday Park – ℡ 08 9841 3593, 1800 644 674, big4@iinnet.com.au
- Mt Melville Caravan Park – ℡ 08 9841 3593, 1800 888 617
- Panorama Caravan Park & Holiday Cottages – ℡ 08 9844 4580
- Rose Gardens Beachside Holiday Park – ℡ 08 9844 1868, 1800 889 999, www.acclaimparks.com.au

Coastal Parks near Albany

Some of the region's most spectacular coastline is included within national parks and nature reserves near Albany. CALM's district office in Albany can answer most inquiries on these areas.

West Cape Howe National Park
(Map p124, J5)

About 30 km west of Albany, this hilly, 3500ha park features dramatic dolerite sea cliffs, pristine beaches, coastal heath and mature karri forest. Torbay Head is WA's southernmost point.

The park is an adventurer's playground, with sandy 4WD tracks leading to places like **West Cape Howe** (a top rock-climbing venue), **Dunsky Beach** (reef diving and snorkelling), **Golden Gates Beach** (surfing) and **Bornholm Beach** (salmon fishing in season). Beautiful **Shelley Beach**, which is accessible by 2WD vehicles, is arguably the South West's top hang-gliding venue – the launch spot is on the hill above the beach.

Torbay Head, off Shelley Beach, WA's southernmost point

Hang-gliding at Shelley Beach

The Bibbulmun Track traverses the park's full length from Lowlands Beach to **Cosy Corner Beach**, where there's a shire campground just a few steps from Torbay's western shore.

West Cape Howe is managed by rangers based at Torndirrup National Park.

Torndirrup National Park
(Maps pp124 J6 & 125 J7)

Seen from Albany, the rugged peninsula that protects the port from the wild Southern Ocean makes a scenic backdrop to Princess Royal Harbour. This is the setting for the 3900ha Torndirrup National Park, the entrance to which is on Frenchman Bay Rd just 10km from town. The park includes massive granite outcrops, peppermint and banksia woodlands and thickets, karri forest, coastal heath and superb coastal views, particularly on the ocean side.

Torndirrup has some excellent opportunities for outdoor pursuits such as fishing, rock climbing (on **Peak Head** and The Amphitheatre, near **The Gap**), bushwalking and swimming. Major attractions include the Whale World Museum and scenic draws such as **Natural Bridge** (a wave-sculpted arch in granite) and the **Blow Holes** (aurally very impressive in a heavy swell). **Salmon Holes** is a popular surfing and fishing spot, while nearby **Misery Beach** offers safe swimming. Sealed roads provide access to most of these places.

Exhilarating scenery is a feature of the 10km return walk from the Isthmus Hill car park to **Bald Head**. The walk isn't particularly difficult, but it's not a leisurely stroll, either – it takes at least six hours to complete, and long trousers are recommended to protect your legs from the prickly vegetation. The 500m **Stony Hill Walk** offers panoramic views from the park's highest point.

The ranger's office (✆ 08 9844 4090) is on Frenchman Bay Rd near the park entrance.

Two Peoples Bay Nature Reserve
(Map p125, H8)

The intriguing name of this picturesque feature, which is about 35km east of Albany, recalls an unexpected encounter between French explorers and American sealers that took place here in 1802. To commemorate the event the meeting place was named *Baie des Deux Peuples*, since anglicised to Two Peoples Bay.

RAY MARTIN

Natural Bridge

Today, however, the area is known more for its association with the **noisy scrub-bird**. Once thought to be extinct, this diminutive, almost-flightless songster was rediscovered here by a bird-watcher in 1961. The area was slated for residential development at the time. One thing led to another and, with the timely support of Prince Philip, one of Australia's first conservation battles was won. Since then the number of noisy scrub-birds has increased dramatically and they have been reintroduced to other reserves with suitable habitat.

In 1994 Two Peoples Bay was the scene of another major rediscovery when a **Gilbert's potoroo** – a rabbit-sized rat-kangaroo that had also long been presumed extinct – was found in the 4700ha reserve. Other endangered mammals known to occur here include the quokka (of Rottnest Island fame), the quenda (a bandicoot) and the western ringtail possum.

The rich diversity of heaths, woodlands, wetlands and coastal shorelines has resulted in 188 bird species (70% of them resident) being recorded here. Not surprisingly, the reserve is a magnet for nature lovers, who come to observe the wildlife and, hopefully, catch a glimpse of its famous rarities. See Bird-Watching pp 27-28.

Other attractions include **Little Beach** (a pretty swimming spot) and the Baie des Deux Peuples Heritage Walk (a 2km-long discovery of the reserve's history and plant life).

ROB VAN DRIESUM

Frenchman Bay

You can learn more about the local wildlife in the reserve's excellent visitor centre – it opens from 10am to 3pm daily in summer, less frequently at other times. For information, contact the ranger on © 08 9846 4276.

Waychinicup National Park
(Map p125, G9)

This 4700ha coastal park, 68km east of Albany, features stunning coastal scenery, views of **Mt Manypeaks**, spring wildflowers and stunning **Waychinicup Inlet**. The latter is reached by a 6km dirt road off Cheyne Beach Rd, which links the park's eastern end to the South Coast Hwy. Otherwise vehicle access is limited to 4WD tracks that lead to fishing spots along the coast. This is another good spot to catch a glimpse of many of the South West's threatened or endangered wildlife species.

The coastal heathland on and around the steep slopes of Mt Manypeaks is considered among WA's most diverse in terms of its plant species. Unfortunately, this fascinating area has had to be closed even to bushwalkers in order to prevent the spread of dieback.

Waychinicup is managed by rangers based at Two Peoples Bay.

Where to Stay

You have a choice of Cheynes Beach Caravan Park (© 08 9846 1247, cheynes_cp@west net.com.au) or the small but delightful campground (tents only) at Waychinicup Inlet.

Flowering grass tree, Waychinicup NP

Mt Barker (Map p124, E5)

This friendly farming community, on Albany Hwy 47km north of Albany, makes a good base from which to explore the district's wineries and the Porongurup and Stirling Range national parks. The Mt Barker Tourist Bureau (© 08 9851 1919, mtbarkwa@comswest.net.au) on Albany Hwy is an excellent source of local information.

Banksia Farm (© 08 9851 1770) on Pearce Rd has gardens displaying all 76 species of *Banksia* and over 90 species of *Dryandra*. Guided tours cost $11 and take at least an hour.

Waychinicup River Inlet, a delightful place to camp

Where to Stay

There's quite a bit of accommodation in the Mt Barker district including these budget places:

- Chill Out Backpackers – Mt Barker (℡ 08 9851 2798)
- Mt Barker Caravan Park – Mt Barker (℡ 08 9851 1691)
- Porongurup Range Tourist Park – Porongurup (℡ 08 9853 1057)

Porongurup National Park
(Maps pp124 F6 & 125 F7)

The 2620ha Porongurup National Park, 40km north of Albany, encompasses one of WA's most outstanding scenic features: the Porongurup Range. You'll see this remarkable island of soaring bluffs as you drive along the Albany Hwy between Albany and Mt Barker, and won't be able to resist a closer look.

The park's most obvious features are the huge granite domes that tower above the surrounding plain. Surprisingly, given the drier nature of the country here, much of the range is covered in karri forest. A remnant of former wetter times, the trees survive here by virtue of the moister local microclimate. The park has 750 plant species including more than 65 orchids.

The ranger station (℡ 08 9853 1095) is at the park's main entrance on Bolganup Rd, near Porongurup.

What to See & Do

Road access within the park is limited, but there are plenty of good walks you can do through the forests and rock formations.

Several tracks leave from the **'Tree in the Rock'** picnic area, which is set among tall karri trees at the end of Bolganup Rd. The name comes from a mature karri that grows from the top of a large granite outcrop about 100m from the information shelter.

One such walk is the 800m Bolganup Heritage Trail, an easy introduction to the local flora and fauna. More testing is the Nancy Peak Walk, a strenuous, 5.5km circuit that includes the summits of **Hayward Peak**, **Nancy Peak** and **Morgan's View**. It takes at least two hours and the views are worth it, with the ragged blue outline of the Stirling Range 40km to the north; on a clear day you can see the ocean.

At the park's eastern end, the **Castle Rock Walk** (4km return, two hours) takes you past a

The Stirling Range looms in the distance from Porongurup NP

The granite domes of Porongurup National Park

Tree in the Rock

huge balancing rock and up to the castle summit. The final stage of this walk is classified as difficult.

Castle Rock is an occasional venue for abseiling and rock climbing, as are **Gibraltar Rock** and **Marmabup Peak**. Gibraltar Rock has routes to suit all levels of expertise, while the others are mainly for experienced climbers. Paragliding is possible off Nancy Peak and Morgan's View, but gliders must have a permit.

Stirling Range walking track

Where to Stay

Camping is not permitted within the park, but the Porongurup Range Tourist Park is just a short drive from the main entrance. There is plenty of alternative accommodation in the area; the Mt Barker Tourist Bureau has details.

Stirling Range National Park
(Maps pp124 D6 & 125 D7-D9)

The 116,000ha Stirling Range National Park, in gently undulating farming country about 80km north of Albany, boasts a spectacular topography of high bluffs, peaks and ridges that is quite different to anything else you'll see in the South West. The park is also noted for its incredibly rich diversity of native flora.

The Stirling Range straddles Chester Pass Rd, the main route between Albany and Gnowangerup. Most of the park's roads are gravel and there are many loose corners. Drive carefully.

Remember too that weather conditions within the range can change rapidly and unexpectedly, particularly in spring – hypothermia and dehydration (or worse) are real dangers here. Carry plenty of water, dress sensibly and always be prepared for wind chill, rain and low clouds. The best time to visit is September to early December, when the days are warming up and the wildflowers are at their best.

The moody Stirling Range

Information

Contact the park rangers (☏ 08 9827 9230 or 9827 9278) for expert advice on walks and other activities. One ranger is based at the Bluff Knoll turn-off and the other at Moingup Springs in Chester Pass. Hikers must register before attempting the longer routes; abseilers and climbers are required to register their intentions in the log book at the Bluff Knoll turn-off.

What to See & Do

The botanical wealth to be found in these ranges is extraordinary. Over 1500 species of plants have been recorded, including around 82 that occur nowhere else – there are 123 species of orchids alone. In late spring even the hardy thickets that cover the higher peaks are ablaze with wildflowers. Such floristic abundance is due firstly to the range being cooler and moister than the surrounding countryside, and secondly to the different microclimates found within the hills.

Thanks to the diversity of plants and landforms there is also a diversity of birds – 140 species have been recorded, 90 of which breed within the park. Good spots for bird-watching include **White Gum Flats** (on Stirling Range Drive) and the **Moingup Springs Campsite**.

Apart from wildflowers, the park's main draw is the challenge of **Bluff Knoll**, which at 1095m is the South West's highest point. For walkers the summit is 3km along a marked route from the parking area – the ascent is of medium difficulty and takes at least two hours. There's a great sense of achievement when you finally reach the top, and, as you'd expect, the views are superb.

The soaring, 300m-high north face of Bluff Knoll is a famous venue for climbing. The rock here is shale-quartzite and is no place for novices. Most of the routes take at least six hours to complete. For safety reasons abseiling is not permitted on the north face.

Seen on an overcast day, the dark, brooding bulk of **Toolbrunup Peak** (1050m) has a menacing quality, like something out of *The Lord of the Rings*. You can climb to the summit from the car park on the eastern side – it's a hard slog

Toolbrunup Peak

DENIS O'BYRNE

Goanna on the road, Stirling Range NP (that's Baby Barnett Hill in the background)

ROB VAN DRIESUM

Bluff Knoll

ROB BOEGHEIM

that gets progressively steeper, but the views are terrific. Allow at least three hours for the 4km return walk.

Other major peaks with marked routes to the top include **Mt Magog** (6km return; four hours), **Talyuberlup Peak** (2.5km return; 2 hours), **Mt Hassell** (3km return; two hours) and **Mt Trio** (3km return; two hours). The Mt Magog route is classified as hard, while the others are of medium difficulty.

The Stirling Range Retreat sells a booklet by AT Morphet that describes the **Stirling Ridge Walk**, a 20km cross-country route from Ellen Peak to Bluff Knoll. The route is unmarked and often difficult, and takes two to three days to complete, but is well worth the effort.

Note that some areas, such as Mondurup Peak, are closed to protect rare flora from dieback infection. Check with the ranger before doing any walks off the beaten track.

Clouds rolling over Ellen Peak

Organised Tours

The Stirling Range Retreat (☏ 08 9827 9229, www.stirlingrange.com.au), on Chester Pass Rd near the Bluff Knoll turn-off, has a couple of good, daily tours in season. Bird walks ($15) operate at dusk and dawn from mid-September to 31 October, and wildflower tours ($22) specialising in orchids run from 1 September to 31 October.

Where to Stay

There are a handful of places close to the action where you can park a caravan and/or pitch a tent. The Mt Barker Visitor Centre has details of other accommodation options in the area. Try the following:

- Moingup Springs – Chester Pass Rd; managed by CALM.
- Stirling Range Retreat – Chester Pass Rd (☏ 08 9827 9229, www.stirlingrange.com.au)
- Trio Park Bush Camp – off Salt River Rd (☏ 08 9827 9270, triopark@westnet.com.au)

Kojonup (Map p120, H3)

Kojonup, a small farming community on the Albany Hwy 253km from Perth, is a good place to break your journey. It was established as a military outpost in 1837 and its attractions include a barracks that dates back to 1845. The Kojonup Visitor Centre (☏ 08 9831 0500) is at 143 Albany Hwy.

What to See & Do

Several small nature reserves in the area protect remnant patches of bush including woodlands of she-oak and wandoo, and all offer good potential for bird-watching and wildflowers in season. They include the 250ha **Farrar Nature Reserve**, about 15km west of town, which you can walk to along an old railway alignment – check at the visitor centre for the latest on cycle access. Forty-six km northwest of town, **Lake Towerrining** is a large freshwater lake that's good for canoeing and bird-watching.

Kojonup also has the famous **Australian Rose Maze**. While you're wandering around getting lost you can learn about Kojonup's history through the stories of three fictional Kojonup women – one of British descent, one Italian and one Nyoongar.

Fitzgerald River National Park (Map p126, H2-H3)

This 329,000ha park, 180km northeast of Albany, features a beautiful coastline of small coves and long surf beaches interspersed with rocks and high cliffs. Inland, scattered quartzite peaks dominate vast rolling heathlands that are renowned for their staggering floristic diversity. Early explorers and farmers dismissed the area as 'worthless', yet it has been determined that the park, which covers a mere 0.1% of the state's surface, contains around 15% of its woody plant species. Nearly 1900 species have been recorded, including 75 endemics and another 250 that are either rare or restricted to the area. Not surprisingly, the park is considered one of the nation's most botanically significant areas.

As well, the park is home to 22 mammal species, more than any other park in the South West. The 184 bird species that have been recorded here include several WA endemics such as the red-capped parrot, red-eared firetail and western thornbill; endemic subspecies include the western ground parrot and western bristle-bird, both of which are endangered. The threatened mallee fowl can often be seen at the Four Mile Beach Campsite during the breeding season.

About one-quarter of the park is classified as wilderness (foot traffic only); several hills have been closed to walkers above the 150m contour line in an attempt to prevent the spread of dieback (see p14).

All major roads within the park are gravel and may be closed in wet weather. A number of coastal spots are accessible to 4WD vehicles only.

Information

The park headquarters (☏ 08 9835 5043) is on Quiss Rd near the South Coast Hwy, about 19km east of Jerramungup. Rangers are also based at East Mt Barren in the east, and on Murray Rd in the southwest.

What to See & Do

Naturally, admiring the wildflowers is popular with all visitors. Mid to late spring is best, but there are interesting flowers to be seen throughout the year. In the park's east, the **Hamersley Drive Heritage Trail** (with accompanying brochure) introduces some of the area's more unusual plants. Strangest of all is the royal hakea, which from a distance has a classic cactus shape. Its variegated leaves grow in dense columns and feature all the colours of the spectrum. Another is the Quaalup bell, a sparse shrub with large, pendulous, beautifully coloured flower heads. The dense clawflower – a small, pine-like plant with dense, mauve, claw-like blooms – and the veined jugflower are other distinctive plants.

Late autumn to late spring is the whale-watching season, and **Point Ann**, which has been developed with picnic shelters, a campground and whale-watching platform, is a particularly good spot to do it in. Humpbacks are uncommon, but on a good day you'll see a dozen or more adult southern rights and their newborn calves quite close to shore.

There are several walking tracks ranging from short and easy (**Mt Maxwell**, 100m) to longer and more strenuous (**East Mt Barren**, 4km return). The latter is a great vantage point for coastal views, as is the summit of **West Mt Barren** (3km return). As well, there's good potential for coastal walks and treks along management tracks in the wilderness zone. Hikers intending to indulge in longer walks should register their intentions with the rangers.

Royal hakea, also known as Chinese lantern bush, is the only native Western Australian plant with variegated leaves

South Coast

Generally speaking, the park's 4WD tracks are only suitable for vehicles with good ground clearance and low-range gearing. In the east you can visit the **Hamersley Dunes**, **Whalebone Beach** and rugged **Quoin Head**, all of which are reached off Hamersley Drive. The Hamersley Dunes are only suitable for drivers skilled in soft sand; the tracks to Whalebone Beach and Quoin Head are slow and rough, but the stunning scenery and sense of isolation make the tedium worthwhile.

Whalebone Beach

In the central south a 4WD track off Pabelup Drive leads to **Fitzgerald Inlet**, where woodlands of medium-sized trees provide a contrast to low mallee scrub and heath. The inlet is a good spot to observe water birds and to fish for black bream. Experienced off-road drivers can continue past the campground to **Fitzgerald Beach**, which is drivable for 4-5km. There are good surf-fishing spots here as well as further south at Point Ann – tracks on either side of the point provide 4WD access onto **Point Charles Bay Beach** and **Trigelow Beach**.

Where to Stay

Within the national park there are bush campgrounds along the coast at St Marys Inlet (near Point Ann), Fitzgerald Inlet (4WD), Quoin Head (4WD), Hamersley Inlet and Four Mile Beach. You can also pitch a tent at the historic Quaalup Homestead (✆ 08 9837 4124) at the park's western end. Otherwise there are caravan parks in Bremer Bay (✆ 08 9837 4018) and Hopetoun (✆ 08 9838 3096), both of which are small coastal townships on the edge of the national park.

Ravensthorpe (Map p126, G3)

This historic mining town grew out of the gold rush days of the 1890s and is the major resupply centre for extended visits into the Fitzgerald River National Park. Sections totalling 38km of the alignment of the now-dismantled railway between Ravensthorpe and Hopetoun have been developed for walkers – the tourist bureau (✆ 08 9838 1277) on Morgans St has brochures.

There's good potential for fossicking in the nearby Ravensthorpe Range, but be careful not to trespass on private property. The tourist bureau has a large display of 72 minerals that have been collected locally.

Where to Stay

Budget accommodation is available at the following places:

- Palace Hotel & Backpackers –
  ✆ 08 9838 1005
- Ravensthorpe Caravan Park –
  ✆ 08 9838 1050
- Ravensthorpe Motel – ✆ 08 8938 1053

The historic Port Hotel in Hopetoun

Showy banksia (Banksia speciosa) *was first collected from the Esperance area*

Esperance Coast

Much of the coast east of the Fitzgerald River National Park is one stunningly beautiful beach after another, and as often as not the only footprints will be your own. Here you'll find some great opportunities for bird-watching, bush camping, bushwalking, canoeing, kayaking, scuba diving and whale-watching, while the extensive kwongan heathlands are an absolute delight in spring. These activities mainly centre on Stokes, Cape Le Grand and Cape Arid national parks. The Archipelago of the Recherche, which stretches over 200km along the coast from Esperance to Cape Arid, contains over 100 islands and 1500 islets. It forms one of Australia's most captivating seascapes.

Stokes National Park
(Map p126, G5-H5)

This coastal park, about 70km west of Esperance, covers 10,700ha of mainly undulating mallee heath interspersed with patches of taller paper-bark and yate in wetland areas. Its coastline is often spectacular, with live dunes and tall, craggy limestone cliffs towering over long, white beaches. The major activities available here are beach and estuary fishing, bird-watching, bush-walking, camping, four-wheel driving, scuba diving, snorkelling and surfing.

Access to the coast is by foot or 4WD vehicle only, but the main attraction – picturesque **Stokes Inlet** – is readily accessible by a good gravel road. Note that all 4WD tracks have sections of deep sand, and vehicles that lack good ground clearance and/or low-range gearing are unlikely to get through.

The ranger's office (✆ 08 9076 8541) is off the main access road and just inside the park's northern boundary.

What to Do

Most visitors come to the park intending to catch a feed of the **black bream** that thrive in the inlet's shallow waters. On an average day you're almost guaranteed success, although as is so often the case there's a lot of water mixed up with the big ones.

Stokes Inlet covers 12 sq km and is actually the estuary for the Young and Lort rivers. It's a good spot to see water birds and waders, with around 30 species having been recorded here and at nearby **Lake Coobinup**.

Normally you can canoe about 3km up the scenic **Young River** from where it enters the estuary. The river is very attractive, with tall vegetation and granite outcrops lining its banks. It's another good place to catch bream and observe the wildlife.

Starting at the car park on Stokes Inlet, the **Stokes Heritage Trail** (6km return) offers nice views of the inlet and a profusion of wild-flowers in season. About half of the track is suitable for wheelchairs.

The other main area of interest centres on beautiful **Fanny Cove**. Reached by a 4WD track off Farrells Rd in the east, it boasts a sheltered bay and the usual long white beach. Salmon, shark, skippy, mulloway and herring are common catches both here and at Skippy Rock, in the park's extreme west. **Skippy Rock** offers good snorkelling as well.

About 2km south of the Fanny Cove Campsite is one of the better surfing breaks in the Esperance area; it's at its best on winter high tides. At nearby **Shoal Cape** an outstanding scuba-diving spot features an idyllic inner lagoon (perfect for snorkellers) ringed by a limestone reef that plunges 19m on the ocean side. Strong currents in the channel between the inner and outer reef make it suitable for experienced and accompanied divers only.

Also near Fanny Cove are the substantial stone ruins of **Moir Homestead**. Established by the Moir brothers in the 1870s, it is fast crumbling away and conservation work is planned to arrest the decay.

Where to Stay

There are two campgrounds with good shelter and caravan access by the inlet. You can also camp at Fanny Cove and Skippy Rock, although these areas are very small.

Esperance (Map p126, H6)

A major regional centre and export-shipping terminal, Esperance (pop 12,000) is the largest town on the southern Australian coast between Albany and Port Lincoln, in South Australia. It's the hub of a prosperous agricultural hinterland, with commercial fishing and tourism being other important industries. The coastal parks in this area are all close enough to town to be visited on day trips, and there are plenty of organised trips available.

South Coast

Esperance Region Tourism Association

Twilight Bay

Rob Boegheim

Pink Lake

Esperance Region Tourism Association

Snorkelling at Woody Island

Rob Boegheim

The tanker jetty, Esperance

Information

The friendly and efficient Esperance visitor centre (✆ 1300 664 455, www.visitesperance .com) is in the Historic Village on Dempster St. CALM's district office (✆ 08 9071 3733) at 92 Dempster St can tell you about the local parks and reserves.

What to See & Do

The beaches near town offer some good potential for water sports. **Twilight Bay** has safe swimming, **Fourth Beach** and **Observatory Beach** are popular windsurfing spots, while **West Beach**, Fourth Beach and Observatory Beach all have good surfing breaks.

A short drive north of town, the 3400ha **Lake Warden Wetlands** encompasses seven major lakes (including the aptly named **Pink Lake**) and numerous smaller ones that provide resting, feeding and breeding habitats for thousands of water birds and migratory waders. In fact, the conservation value of this system is so high that it has been listed under the international Ramsar Convention. You can learn all about it on a 3.6km (one-way) walking track with information panels and bird hides en route.

A little further out, the **Monjingup Nature Reserve** is another good spot for bird-watching as well as wildflowers.

Xanadu Horse Rides (✆ 08 9075 9029) has tailor-made trail rides of up to one day on a farm adjoining Cape Le Grand Beach. Meals can be provided, and you can camp there.

Esperance's most obvious scenic feature is the magnificent **Archipelago of the Recherche**, whose peaked islands dominate the view southwards of town. The islands are nature reserves and the only one that visitors can land on without a permit is **Woody Island.** Bird-watching, bushwalking, fishing and snorkelling are popular activities here. You can get to Woody Island daily with Mackenzies Island Cruises (✆ 08 9071 5757), which runs 'eco-stays' on the island.

Scuba divers come from far and wide to dive the wreck of the *Sanko Harvest*, a huge bulk carrier that sank after running onto rocks in 1991. Unbelievably, the captain had attempted to traverse the archipelago at night. The wreck is in three pieces between 14m and 42m down, 38km from Esperance. Otherwise there are literally hundreds of good dive sites among the islands that feature spectacular underwater topography and marine life. The **tanker jetty** in town is a great place to see myriad small fish, sea dragons and colourful corals and sponges. Esperance Diving & Fishing (✆ 08 9071 5111, www.esperancedivingandfishing.com.au) does dive trips.

Fishing is hugely popular and the visitor centre has a list of 30 places with access notes and common species. See p36 for details of local fishing charters.

Esperance Eco-Discovery Tours (✆ 0407 737 261, www.esperancetours.com.au) offers tag-along 4WD day trips to remote tracks and beaches around Esperance ($95 per vehicle).

Adventure Pursuits (✆ 0403 009 620) takes sand-boarding trips and will teach you how to abseil from a 22m-high cliff. The Esperance Surfing Academy (✆ 08 9071 1432) offers surfing tuition.

Scenic flights, 4WD tours and whale-watching and island cruises are also available.

Where to Stay

Woody Island Eco-Stays (✆ 08 9071 5757, www.woodyisland.com.au) has accommodation in a range of mostly budget venues from September to April, or you can pitch your own tent. There are several other budget places in town:

- Bathers Paradise Caravan Park – ✆ 08 9071 1014, batherscpark@wn.com.au
- Blue Waters Lodge YHA – ✆ 08 9071 1040
- Crokers Park Holiday Resort – ✆ 08 9071 4100, crokerspark@bigpond.com.au
- Esperance Backpackers – ✆ 08 9071 4724
- Esperance Bay Caravan Park – ✆ 08 9071 2237
- Esperance Guest House – ✆ 08 9071 3396
- Esperance Seafront Caravan Park – ✆ 08 9071 1251, www.esperanceseafront.com
- Pink Lake Tourist Park – ✆ 1800 011 311, www.pinklakepark.com.au

Cape Le Grand National Park
(Map p127, H7)

This 32,100ha park, 50km east of Esperance, features spectacular coastal scenery and rolling heathlands dominated by scattered granite hills. The major activities available here are beach fishing, beach driving, walking, camping and swimming. Almost all visitors confine themselves to the park's western end, where good roads (mostly sealed) provide access to sweeping surf beaches and sheltered coves.

The place names here are like the pages of a history book. In 1792 the French explorer Admiral D'Entrecasteaux named Cape Le Grand after one of his officers. **Lucky Bay** recalls a visit by Matthew Flinders in 1802 – he was lucky to find shelter here from a wild summer storm. Flinders named **Thistle Cove** after John Thistle, master of HMS *Endeavour*. Finally, the explorer Edward John Eyre named **Rossiter Bay** after the master of the *Mississippi*, which he found anchored in the bay at the end of his historic trek from Adelaide.

The ranger's office (✆ 08 9075 9072, 0429 041 067) is beside the main access road just beyond the fee collection point.

What to See & Do

In the park's southwest corner is a chain of granite hills, the highest of which are **Mt Le Grand** (345m) and the distinctive **Frenchmans Peak** (262m). You can climb the latter from the car park on its southeastern side. Getting to the top

Whistling Rock at Thistle Cove

ROB VAN DRIESUM

is hard work on a long, steep slope, but the stunning views of the coast and islands make it well worthwhile. Allow two hours for the return journey. **Mississippi Point** at the southern end of Rossiter Bay also offers great views.

Another worthwhile exercise is to walk the 15km Coastal Trail from **Le Grand Beach** to Rossiter Bay. This trek, which varies from easy to hard going, connects a series of beautiful coves – **Hellfire Bay**, Thistle Cove and Lucky Bay. The walk takes about eight hours one-way, or you can do it in sections. Le Grand Beach, Hellfire Bay and Lucky Bay all offer safe swimming.

Beach fishing yields salmon, herring, skippy, whiting and mulloway – good spots to try include Hellfire Bay, Le Grand Beach and **Dunn Rocks**. You can drive right along the beach from Cape Le Grand to Wylie Bay (near Esperance), a distance of about 23km. Dunn Rocks is accessible either by road or along the beach from the vehicle entry point near Mississippi Hill. These beaches are closed by boggy conditions between May and November.

The park's eastern end includes part of **Wharton's Beach**, which must be one of WA's most beautiful beaches. The view from the granite hills at its eastern end is simply magnificent – and there's not a beach shack or high-rise in sight. To get there, turn off Fisheries Rd at the tiny township of **Congdinup**. En route you pass the almost equally scenic **Duke of Orleans Bay**.

Where to Stay

There are sheltered campgrounds with toilets and showers at Lucky Bay and Le Grand Beach. Both are suitable for caravans.

The Orleans Bay Caravan Park (℗ 08 9075 0033, orleansbay@wn.com.au) is by Duke of Orleans Bay on the road to Whartons Beach.

Cape Arid National Park
(Map p127, G8/9-H8/9)

This large (280,000ha) park 120km east of Esperance features vast heathlands, an exceptionally scenic coastline, and a great sense of space. The main activities available here are beach fishing, bird-watching, whale-watching, bushwalking, camping and four-wheel driving. Remember that this is a big, isolated area and visitors planning to explore its remoter parts should be self sufficient in everything.

The popular Thomas River estuary in the park's southwest corner is readily accessible on a good gravel road. However, you'll need a 4WD vehicle with good ground clearance to visit almost all other points of interest. All the park's 4WD tracks have sections of rough limestone rock and/or soft sand, and can become impassable for long periods after prolonged heavy rain.

The ranger station (℗ 08 9075 0055) is on the road to Dolphin Cove at Thomas River. Leaflets on the park are available from the CALM office in Esperance.

Hellfire Bay

ROB BOEGHEIM

The track to Israelite Bay

What to See & Do

The area around the **Thomas River** estuary has a pleasing variety of plant communities, and these can be explored on several walking tracks between 1km and 7km return. Probably the best one for bird-watchers is the Boolenup Walk (easy; 4km return), which takes you through diverse habitats including a brackish lake. Large zamia palms are an unusual feature of this area.

From June to November the rocks at Thomas River and nearby **Dolphin Cove** are good spots for observing southern right whales and their newborn calves. The mothers can often be seen at close quarters as they give birth in the sheltered water.

There's a great view from Thomas River across **Yokinup Bay** to lofty **Mt Arid**, whose summit offers stunning views of the coast and nearby islands. To get there, drive 18km along the beach to a car park on the mountain's southwestern side, then start climbing!

Yokinup Bay has good beach fishing for skippy, shark, salmon, herring and mulloway. You can expect to catch the same species off the beach at **Poison Creek**, a popular spot for anglers at the western end of Sandy Bight. Poison Creek is accessible to 2WD vehicles with care; with a 4WD you can travel along the beach to **Cape Pasley**, about 16km away at the other end of the bight.

Despite its name, **Thomas Fishery**, on the eastern side of Mt Arid, is not a particularly good fishing spot. However, there's safe swimming in the cove and nearby is the ruin of **Hill Springs Homestead**. It was abandoned in 1910 and today only the stone chimneys remain. Access is 4WD only from the Poison Creek road.

Lonely **Israelite Bay**, in the park's remote eastern section, was the site of a repeater station built in 1876 on the new telegraph line between Perth and the eastern colonies. It was closed in 1927, and various relics such as graves, parts of the old jetty and the station's impressive ruin can still be seen. From here you can drive northwards to the prominent, ragged-topped **Russell Range**, where a marked route leads to the top of Tower Hill (585m). Allow at least two hours for this strenuous jaunt, which gives a fine view of the surrounding mallee.

Where to Stay

There are sheltered bush sites at Mt Ragged (Russell Range) and Thomas River – the main campground at Thomas River has caravan bays. You can also camp at Thomas Fishery, Jorndee Creek and Israelite Bay. ■

ROB VAN DRIESUM

The telegraph station at Israelite Bay

A tannin-stained creek flows into Thistle Cove, Cape Le Grand National Park

Chapter Eight

The Wheatbelt

This gently undulating area east of Perth, with its seemingly endless paddocks and wheat fields, holds a few surprises for those making their way to or from the South West.

Northam (Map p115, B11)

On the western edge of the Wheatbelt, Northam is a regional service centre and transport hub on the Great Eastern Hwy 96km from Perth. It's also a good spot for canoeing, kayaking and hot-air ballooning.

The Northam Visitor Centre (© 08 9622 2100, northam@avon.net.aut) is at 2 Grey St.

What to Do

Northam is on the **Avon River**, and most years between July and September you can canoe all the way from here to Perth. Things go a little crazy during the first weekend in August, when Northam hosts the **Avon Descent**. This is Australia's premier white-water race for canoes/kayaks, skis and powerboats. It's held over two days on 134km of river and includes 45km of white water, 14km of tea-tree thickets and 30km of flat water. If you're interested in an extreme challenge, the official website, www.avondescent.asn.au, will answer most of your questions.

There's also the **Kep Track**, a shared walk/cycle path that will eventually link Northam to Mundaring Weir, in the Perth Hills. At the Northam end the path has been constructed as far as West Northam. The main highlights of this 8km section are picturesque views over the town and Avon Valley.

Northam has the South West's only hot-air balloon operator (see p42).

York & Beverley
(Map p115, C11 & E12)

The first country town in Western Australia, York, 35km south of Northam, is noted for its colonial streetscapes and historic buildings. It's also one of the few places in the South West where you can go parachuting – contact Skydive Express (© 1800 355 833, www.skydive.com.au).

York is on the Great Southern Hwy, 97km east of Perth. Continue south for 33km and you come to the little township of **Beverley**, home of the Beverley Soaring Society (© 0407 385 361, www.beverley-soaring.org.au).

Thirty km west of Beverley, the **Wandoo Conservation Park** is to be expanded into a 43,000ha national park.

Brookton (Map p116, G2)

Brookton, at the intersection of the Great Southern and Brookton highways 33km south of Beverley, is the jumping-off point for visits to the **Boyagin Nature Reserve**. Dominated by tall granite outcrops, this large (nearly 5000ha) patch of remnant bush lies on the boundary of two botanical provinces – the jarrah-marri forests to the west, and the yate-wandoo woodlands to the east. The diversity of plants makes it a good spot for wildflowers and bird-watching.

To get there, head south on the Great Southern Hwy and turn west onto Kulyaling West Rd 11km south of Brookton. The access road ends at a picnic area a short walk from a high granite dome. A Nyoongar myth claims that if you walk to the top without stopping you'll have a long life. Fortunately it's not too difficult a climb. There are no walking tracks in the reserve, but the open nature of the woodland floors makes it easy to get around on foot.

Also worth visiting in this general area is the **Tutanning Nature Reserve**, about 40km southeast of Brookton. This 2000ha reserve contains a good range of habitats including wandoo, casuarina and heath, and a surprising wealth of flora (over 400 species). It's a refuge for many bird species as well as mammals such as kangaroos, numbats, red-tailed phascogales, quendas, tammar wallabies and woylies.

Narrogin (Map p120, B3)

Narrogin, on the western edge of the Wheatbelt 190km from Perth and 136km from Northam, is the commercial and service centre for a large sheep-and-wheat-farming district. It's an attractive town with easy access to the famous

Dryandra Woodland, one of the state's main places for observing native wildlife.

Information

Contact the Narrogin Tourist Bureau (© 08 9881 2064, narrogin.tourist@westnet.com.au) at the corner of Earl and Egerton Sts. CALM's regional office (© 08 9881 1444) is at 7 Wald St.

What to See & Do

There's not much in Narrogin itself in terms of outdoor activities apart from the **Foxes Lair Nature Park**. This patch of remnant bush, opposite the caravan park on Williams Rd, has walks and picnic facilities. Wildflowers are a big attraction in spring.

Head northwest on the Wandering-Narrogin Rd and, after about 30km, you come to the 28,000ha **Dryandra Woodland**. This is not a single entity, but rather a fragmented area of 17 separate bush blocks covered predominantly with wandoo woodlands and plantations of mallet, a local eucalypt once valued for the tannin content of its bark. Most of these blocks are surrounded by ecological wastelands in the form of overcleared wheat paddocks.

Yet Dryandra supports over 100 species of birds and 13 species of mostly small, native ground-dwelling mammals. Several of the latter are considered rare and endangered elsewhere in Australia, including the numbat, tammar wallaby and woylie. Local populations of these three species responded so well to a fox-baiting programme that CALM was inspired to embark on the Return to Dryandra project – an ambitious plan to reintroduce bilbies, boodies, mala, marls and mernines to the woodlands. All these species had disappeared from the Dryandra area since white settlement, but fortunately still clung to survival elsewhere in the state.

As part of this project, which itself forms part of CALM's outstandingly successful Western

Return of the Numbat

At the time of British settlement of Australia, the numbat (*Myrmecobius fasciatus*) occurred across the southern half of Western Australia, through the north of South Australia and into the western part of New South Wales. By the 1980s, however, the state's faunal emblem was restricted to two small populations in the wandoo woodlands of the South West (one of these being at Dryandra) and was staring extinction in the face. Since then it has made a dramatic recovery thanks to CALM's Western Shield programme (see p16), and is now found once more in a number of its former haunts.

Weighing just 500g, and with a head and body length of 250mm, the tiny numbat is a unique creature in more ways than one. First, it is a marsupial without a pouch. Second, it is the only marsupial that has adapted to feeding exclusively on termites. And third, unlike most other marsupials, it is active in the day rather than at night. Another unusual characteristic is its striking markings and colouration. Numbats have a red-brown back marked by transverse white bands, and a greyish white belly and cheeks, the latter distinguished by a black longitudinal stripe through the eye.

Numbats favour wandoo and jarrah areas containing plenty of fallen timber where they can find food and shelter. Having located an underground termite gallery by scent, the numbat, which is not a powerful digger, exposes the gallery by scratching a small hole or turning over a piece of wood. It then uses its long, slender tongue (which moves faster than the eye can see) to extract the termites.

Numbats breed in January and the young, which are born two weeks after mating, are carried on the female's four teats until July when they are transferred to a burrow. They emerge in September, and in December move out to establish their own home territories. Numbat populations are increasing all the time, but the species is still classed as vulnerable to extinction. Hopefully the day is not far off where it will once again be referred to as 'common'.

Shield campaign, a 20ha predator-proof compound was stocked with core populations of the target species, and their offspring released at Dryandra and elsewhere. Carpet pythons and ground-dwelling birds such as quail and mallee fowl have also benefited from fox control.

Almost all Dryandra's native mammals are nocturnal, so without a torch you aren't going to see much. Your best bet is to join an evening tour of the **Barna Mia** breeding compound at **Old Mill Dam** ($12). After a 20-minute talk and slide show, the guide takes you on a 40-minute walk to view the animals at feeding stations along the way. For bookings, ring ☏ 08 9881 9200 on weekdays and 9884 5231 on weekends.

Interesting walks in the area include the 5km Ochre Trail features Nyoongar culture, including an old red ochre mine. CALM's *trail guide* leaflet will point you in the right direction.

Where to Stay

Narrogin has a caravan park (☏ 08 9881 1260), and you can camp at Congelin, on the western edge of the Dryandra Forest off Williams Rd. In the heart of the forest, the Dryandra Settlement (☏ 08 9884 5231) is a restored forestry centre with self-contained cottages and dormitory-style accommodation.

Wave Rock (Map p117, G12)

One of Western Australia's best-known attractions, Wave Rock is 345km east of Perth and 4km from the little town of Hyden. It might seem a long way to drive for a rock, but those who make the effort aren't disappointed.

The formation itself is surreal and the area around it is very pleasant. The 'wave', actually the northern side of Hyden Rock, is about 15m high and 100m long and resembles an enormous dumper about to come crashing down on your head. A remarkable sight! The colourful, vertical stripes are a result of algal growth. The rock also acts as a water catchment for the area, hence the rather ugly concrete barrier along the 'crest'.

Hyden Rock is one of a number of granite outcrops in this area. Other attractions include **Hippo's Yawn**, a gaping, mouth-like opening reached either by car or by a 20-minute walk around the base of Hyden Rock; and **Mulka's Cave**, 25km north, where the walls of an overhang are decorated with ancient hand prints.

Aboriginal culture tours are available at Wave Rock (bookings ☏ 08 9880 5182). The Wave Rock Visitor Centre (☏ 08 9880 5666, www.waverock.com.au) is in the Wildflower Shoppe at Wave Rock.

Where to Stay

It only takes a day at the most to have a good look around, though an overnight stay is worth considering for the different moods of the rock at dusk and dawn. There are several accommodation options in the immediate area:
- Wave-Away Backpackers – ☏ 08 9880 5129
- Wave Rock Resort – ☏ 08 9880 5400
- Wave Rock Motel – ☏ 08 9880 5052, waverockmotel@westnet.com.au
- Wave Rock Caravan Park & Cabins – ☏ 08 9880 5022, waverock@wn.com.au ∎

ROB VAN DRIESUM

Wave Rock

Index

Text References

- **bold** page numbers – major references
- normal page numbers – references (minor references ignored)

Left: Interplay of flora and geology at Cape Leeuwin

Index

Index

Index

Map References

Places/features listed here are those that occur in the above Text References and are shown on the maps – others are not referenced.

They are indicated by map page number followed by grid reference – e.g. "124 H6" means page 124, grid H6.

A

Albany 124 H6,125 H7
Alexandra Bridge 122 B3
Archipelago of the
  Recherche 127 H7-H9
Armadale 115 E7
Augusta 122 C3
Avon River 116 J4-C1,
  115 E12-B8
Avon Valley National Park
  115 A/B8

B

Badgingarra National Park
  110 B4
Balingup 119 H7
Beedelup Falls 123 D7
Beedelup National Park
  123 D7
Beverley 115 E12
Bicentennial Tree 123 E7
Big Brook State Forest
  123 D7
Bindoon 111 J/H8
Black Point 122 D/E6
Blackwood River 122 A6-B3
Bold Park 128 F1-2
Boorara Conservation Park
  123 F9
Boranup Forest 122 B2
Botanic Garden, Western
  Australian 128 F3
Boyagin Nature Reserve
  116 G1
Boyup Brook 119 H9
Bremer Bay 126 J2
Bridgetown 119 J8
Broke Inlet 123 H10

Brookton 116 G2
Bunbury 118 E5
Busselton 118 G4

C

Calgardup Cave 122 B2
Canning River 115 G10-E8
Canning River Regional
  Park 128 G4-H5
Cape Arid National Park
  127 G8/9-H8/9
Cape Leeuwin 122 D3
Cape Le Grand National
  Park 127 H7
Cape Naturaliste 118 F2
Caves Rd 118 G2-J2,
  122 A2-C3
Cervantes 110 C2
Chidlow 115 C8
Circular Pool 123 H12
Cliffy Head 123 H10
Coalmine Beach 123 H11
Collie 119 E8
Collie River 119 G9-D8
Cosy Corner Beach 124 H5
Cottesloe 128 G1
Cowaramup Bay 118 J2

D

Deep River 123 E10-H11
Denmark 124 H4
D'Entrecasteaux National
  Park 122 D5-E6,
  123 E7-H10
D'Entrecasteaux, Point
  123 G7
Diamond Tree 123 C8
Donnelly River 123 B7
Dryandra Woodland
  119 A12
Dunsborough 118 G3
Dwellingup 115 J8

E

Eagle Bay 118 G/F2
Edward Island 110 F3
Ellensbrook Homestead
  118 J2
Esperance 126 H6

F

Fernhook Falls 123 G11
Fitzgerald River National
  Park 126 H2-H3
Frankland River 124 D2-
  123 H12
Fremantle 114 D/E6,
  128 H1

G

Gardner Beach 123 G8
Giants (Mammoth) Cave
  122 B2
Gloucester National Park
  123 D8
Gloucester Tree 123 D8
Gracetown 118 J2
Greenbushes 119 H8
Greens Pool 124 H3
Guilderton 110 H4
Guildford 128 D5

H

Hamelin Bay 122 C2
Hangover Bay 110 C2
Herdsman Lake 128 E2
Hopetoun 126 H3
Hyden 126 E1

I

Israelite Bay 127 G9

J

Jarrahdale 115 F7/8
Jerramungup 121 J12,
  126 H1
Jewel Cave 122 C3
John Forrest National Park
  115 C8
Julimar Conservation Park
  111 J8-J9
Jurien Bay 110 A2

K

Kalamunda 115 D7
Karri Gully 123 A7
King George Sound 125 H7
Kings Park 128 F3
Kojonup 120 H3

South West Western Australia Maps

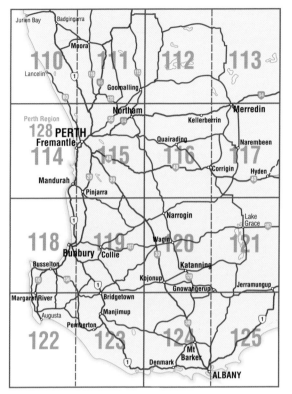

Major Highway/Freeway		
Main Road	sealed	unsealed
Minor Road	sealed unsealed	track
Railway		
Total/Intermediate Kms	★ 98 ★ 36	
National Route/Hwy Number	1 — 94	
State Route Number	30	
Lake, Reservoir		
Intermittent or Salt Lake		
National Park, Nature Res Conservation Reserve		
Conservation Park		
Aboriginal Land / Reserve	YANDEYARRA	
Marine Park		
Homestead	'Hamelin' ■	
Tourist Points of Interest	Gorge •	
Rest Area with Toilet / Water	⊼	
Camping Area	▲	
Bushcamping Area	▲	
Selected Private Camping Area	▲	
Outback Roadhouse	⛽	
Information Centre	i	

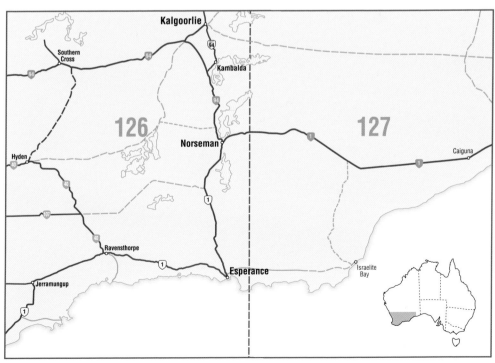

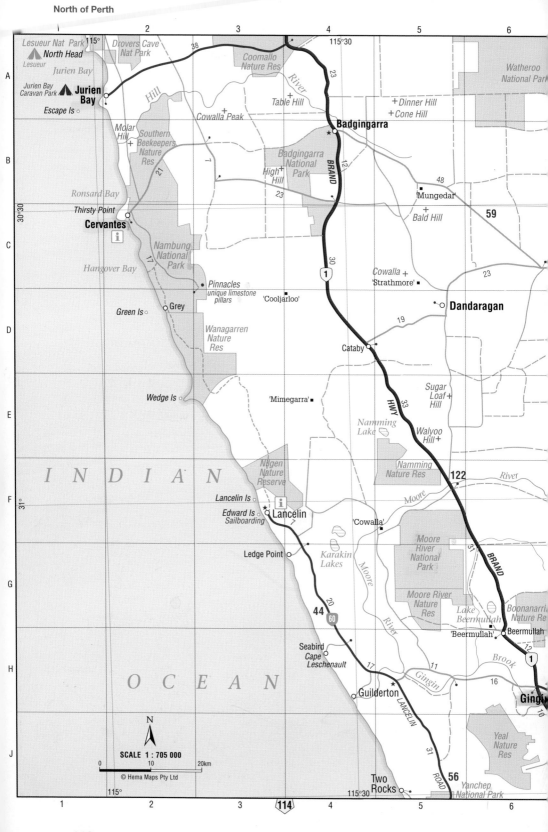

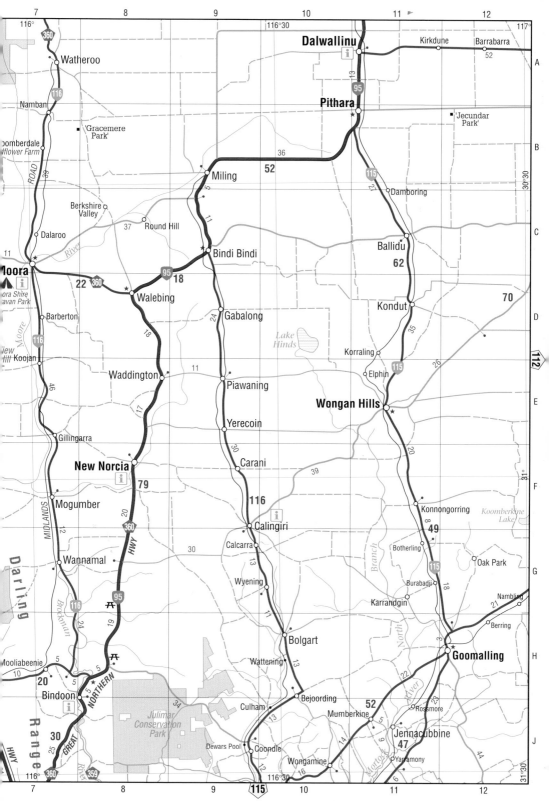

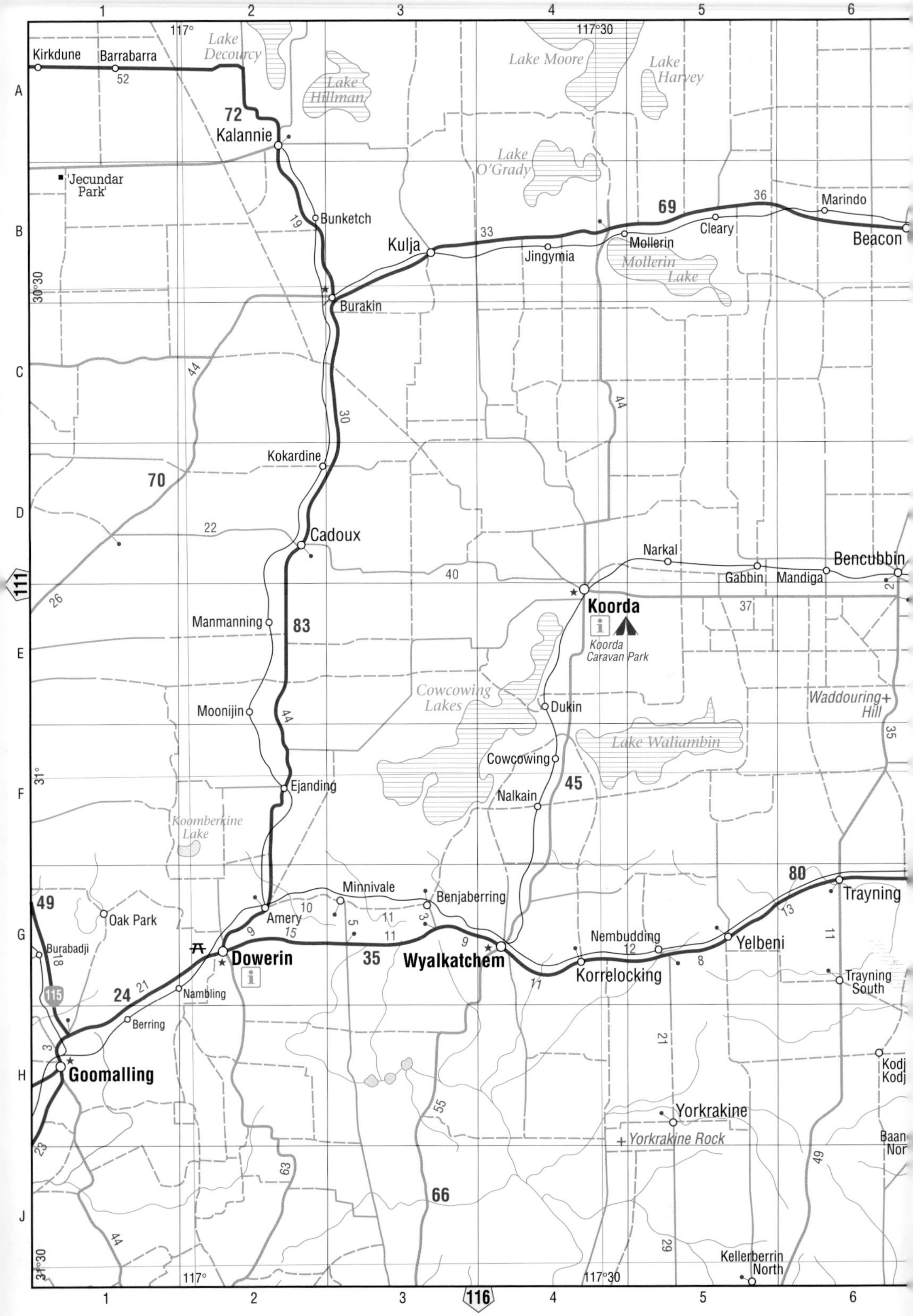

117°
117°30

| | 1 | 2 | 3 | 4 | 5 | 6 |

Kirkdune
Barrabarra
52

Lake
Decourcy
Lake Moore
Lake
Harvey

Lake
Hillman

A

72
Kalannie

'Jecundar
Park'

Lake
O'Grady

30°30

19
Bunketch

69
36
Marindo

Kulja
33
Jingymia
Mollerin
Cleary
Beacon

Mollerin
Lake

B

Burakin

44

30

Kokardine

70

Narkal
Bencubbin

22
Cadoux
40
Gabbin
Mandiga

D

★
Koorda
37

111

26
31°

Manmanning
83

Koorda
Caravan Park

Waddouring
Hill

Moonijin
44

Dukin

Cowcowing
Lakes

Lake Waliambin

35

E

Ejanding

Cowcowing

Koomberkine
Lake

Nalkain
45

F

80
Trayning

49
Oak Park

Minnivale
Benjaberring
13

Burabadji
18
10
Amery
15
9
11
5
11
3
9
Nembudding
12
Yelbeni
11

G
Dowerin
35
Wyalkatchem
11
Korrelocking
8
Trayning
South

24
21
Nambling
Berring

115

21
46

3
Goomalling
H

55

Kodj
Kodj

29

Yorkrakine
Yorkrakine Rock
Baan
Nor

63
66

44
Kellerberrin
North

J

117°
116
117°30
31°30

| | 1 | 2 | 3 | 4 | 5 | 6 |

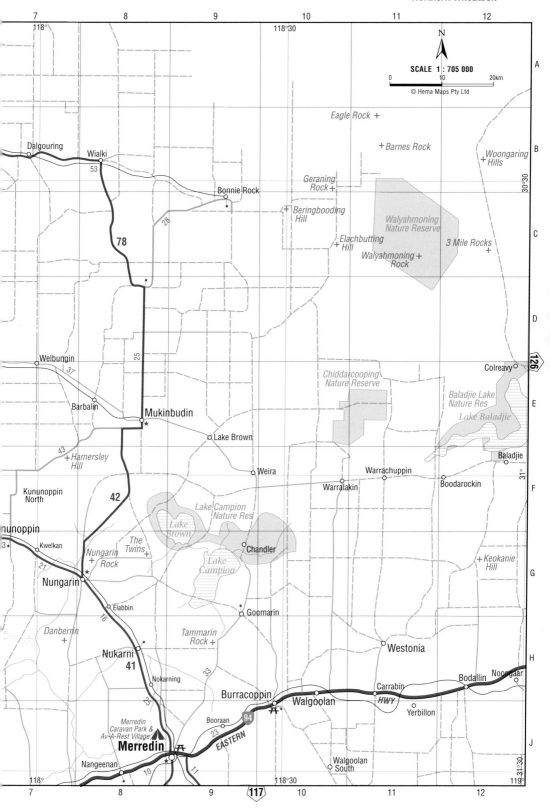

SCALE 1 : 705 000

0   10   20km

© Hema Maps Pty Ltd

Eagle Rock +

+ Barnes Rock

+ Woongaring
  Hills

Dalgouring

Wialki
53

Bonnie Rock

Geraning
Rock +

+ Beringbooding
  Hill

Walyahmoning
Nature Reserve

+ Elachbutting
  Hill

3 Mile Rocks +

Walyahmoning +
Rock

78

28

Welbungin

Colreavy

126

25

Chiddarcooping
Nature Reserve

Baladjie Lake
Nature Res

Barbalin

Mukinbudin

37

Lake Brown

Lake Baladjie

Baladjie

43

+ Hamersley
  Hill

Weira

Warrachuppin

Kununoppin
North

Warralakin

Boodarockin

42

Lake Campion
Nature Res

Kwelkan

Lake
Brown

+ Keokanie
  Hill

21

The
Twins +

Nungarin +
Rock

Chandler

Nungarin

Lake
Campion

Elabbin

Goomarin

16

Danberrin +

Tammarin
Rock +

Westonia

Nukarni

41

Nokarning

Carrabin

Bodallin

Noongaar

25

33

Burracoppin

Walgoolan

HWY

Booraan

94

Yerbillon

Merredin
Caravan Park &
Av-A-Rest Village

23

EASTERN

Merredin

Nangeenan

10

11

Walgoolan
South

117

118°30

119°

113

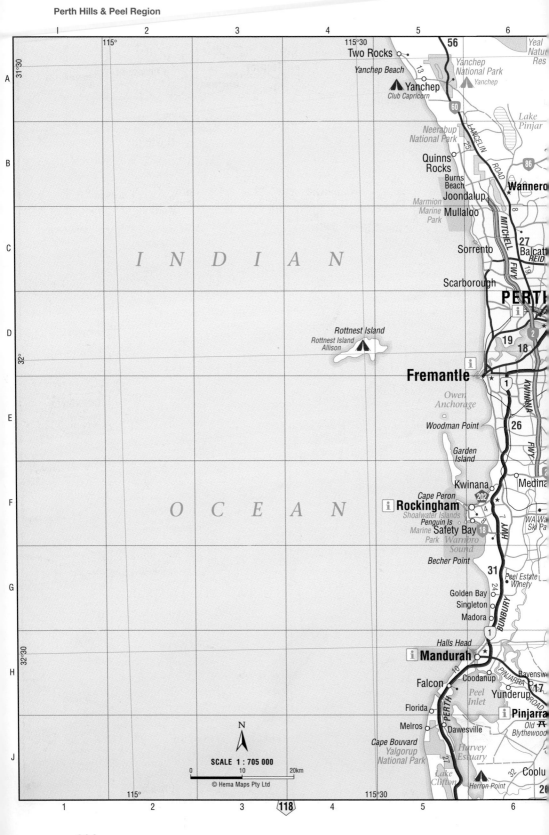

INDIAN

OCEAN

Two Rocks

Yanchep Beach

Yanchep
Club Capricorn

Yeal
Natur
Res

Yanchep
National Park

Yanchep

Lake
Pinjar

Neerabup
National Park

Quinns
Rocks

Burns
Beach

Joondalup

Wannero

Mullaloo

Marmion
Marine
Park

Sorrento

Balcatt

REID

Scarborough

PERTI

Rottnest Island

Rottnest Island
Allison

Fremantle

Owen
Anchorage

Woodman Point

Garden
Island

Kwinana

Medina

Cape Peron

Rockingham

Shoalwater Islands

Penguin Is

Marine

Safety Bay

Park

Warnbro
Sound

Becher Point

Peel Estate
Winery

Golden Bay

Singleton

Madora

Halls Head

Mandurah

Coodanup

Falcon

Bayensw

Peel
Inlet

Yunderup

Florida

Pinjarra

Melros

Old
Blythewoo

Dawesville

Cape Bouvard

Yalgorup
National Park

Harvey
Estuary

Coolu

Lake
Clifton

Herron Point

N

SCALE 1 : 705 000

0   10   20km

© Hema Maps Pty Ltd

115°

115°30

118

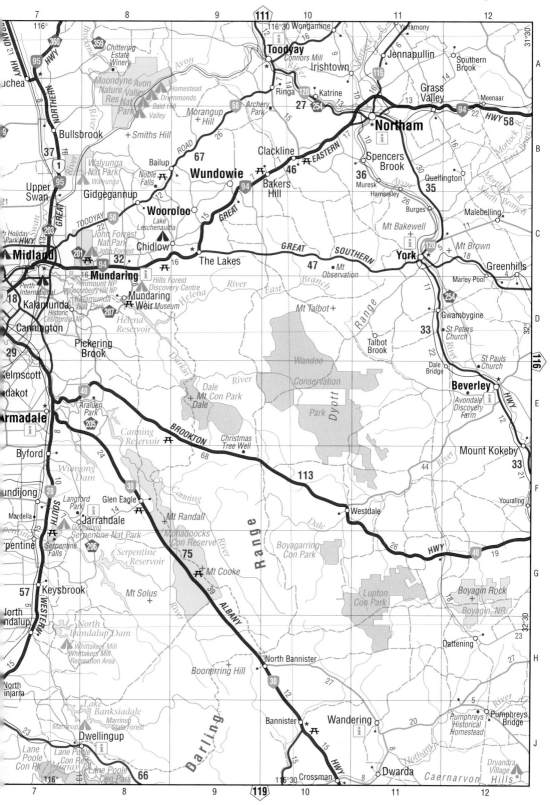

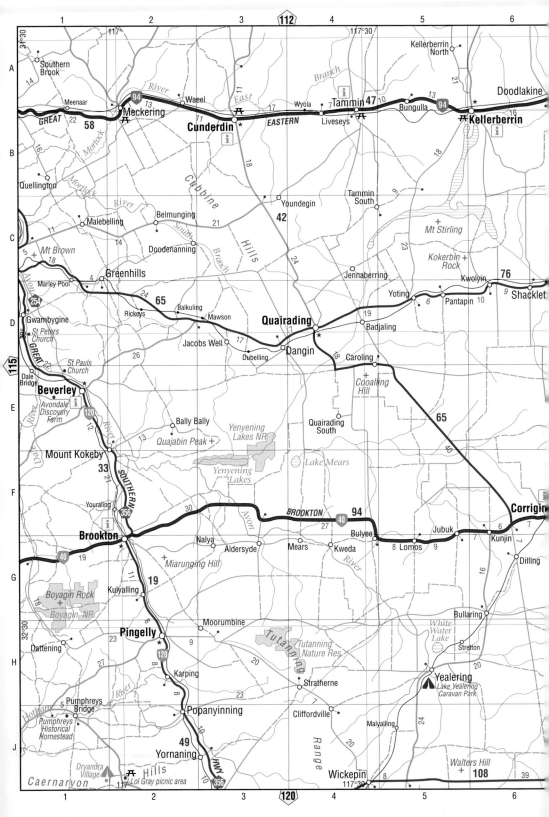

A
- Southern Brook
- Meenaar
- Waeel
- Wyola
- Tammin **47**
- Bungulla
- Kellerberrin North
- Doodlakine
- Meckering
- Cunderdin
- EASTERN
- Liveseys
- Kellerberrin
- **94**
- GREAT **58**
- 94 **13**

B
- Quellington
- Cubbine
- Youndegin
- Tammin South
- Mt Stirling

C
- Malebelling
- Belmunging
- Doodenanning
- **42**
- Jennaberring
- Kokerbin Rock
- Mt Brown
- Marley Pool
- Greenhills
- Yoting
- Pantapin
- Kwolyin
- **76**
- Shacklet
- South Branch Hills

D
- Gwambygine
- St Peters Church
- Rickeys
- Balkuling
- Mawson
- Quairading
- Badjaling
- **65**
- Jacobs Well
- Dubelling
- Dangin
- Caroling
- GREAT
- St Pauls Church
- Dale Bridge

E
- Beverley
- Avondale Discovery Farm
- Bally Bally
- Quajabin Peak
- Yenyening Lakes NR
- Quairading South
- Cooalling Hill
- **65**

F
- Mount Kokeby
- **33**
- Youraling
- Yenyening Lakes
- Lake Mears
- SOUTHERN
- **356**
- Brookton
- Nalya
- Aldersyde
- Mears
- Kweda
- BROOKTON **94**
- Bulyee
- Lomos
- Jubuk
- Kunjin
- Corrigin
- **40**

G
- **40**
- Boyagin Rock
- Boyagin NR
- Kulyalling
- **19**
- Miarunging Hill
- Avon River
- Dilling

H
- Dattening
- Pingelly
- **120**
- Moorumbine
- Karping
- Stratherne
- Tutanning Nature Res.
- White Water Lake
- Bullaring
- Stretton
- Yealering
- Lake Yealering Caravan Park

J
- Pumphreys Bridge
- Pumphreys Historical Homestead
- Popanyinning
- Cliffordville
- Malyalling
- Range
- **49**
- Yornaning
- HWY
- **356**
- Dryandra Village
- Lol Gray picnic area
- Caernarvon Hills
- Wickepin
- Walters Hill **108**

116

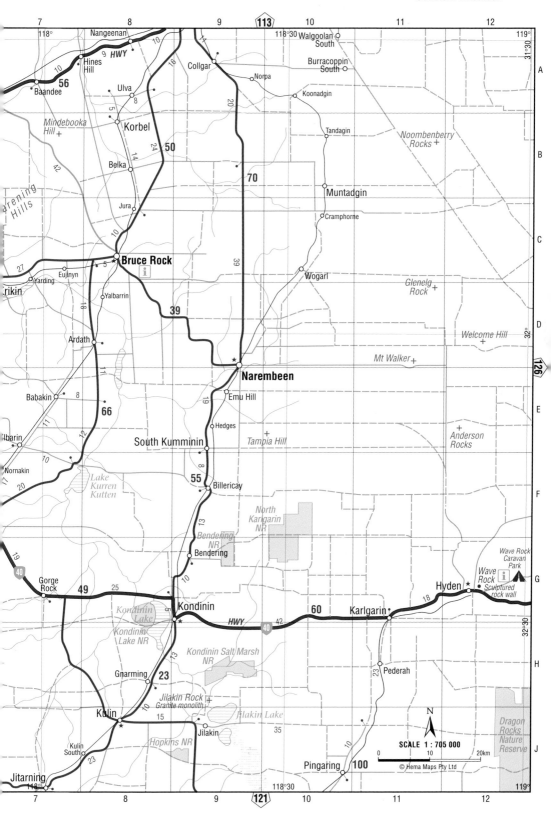

SCALE 1 : 705 000

© Hema Maps Pty Ltd

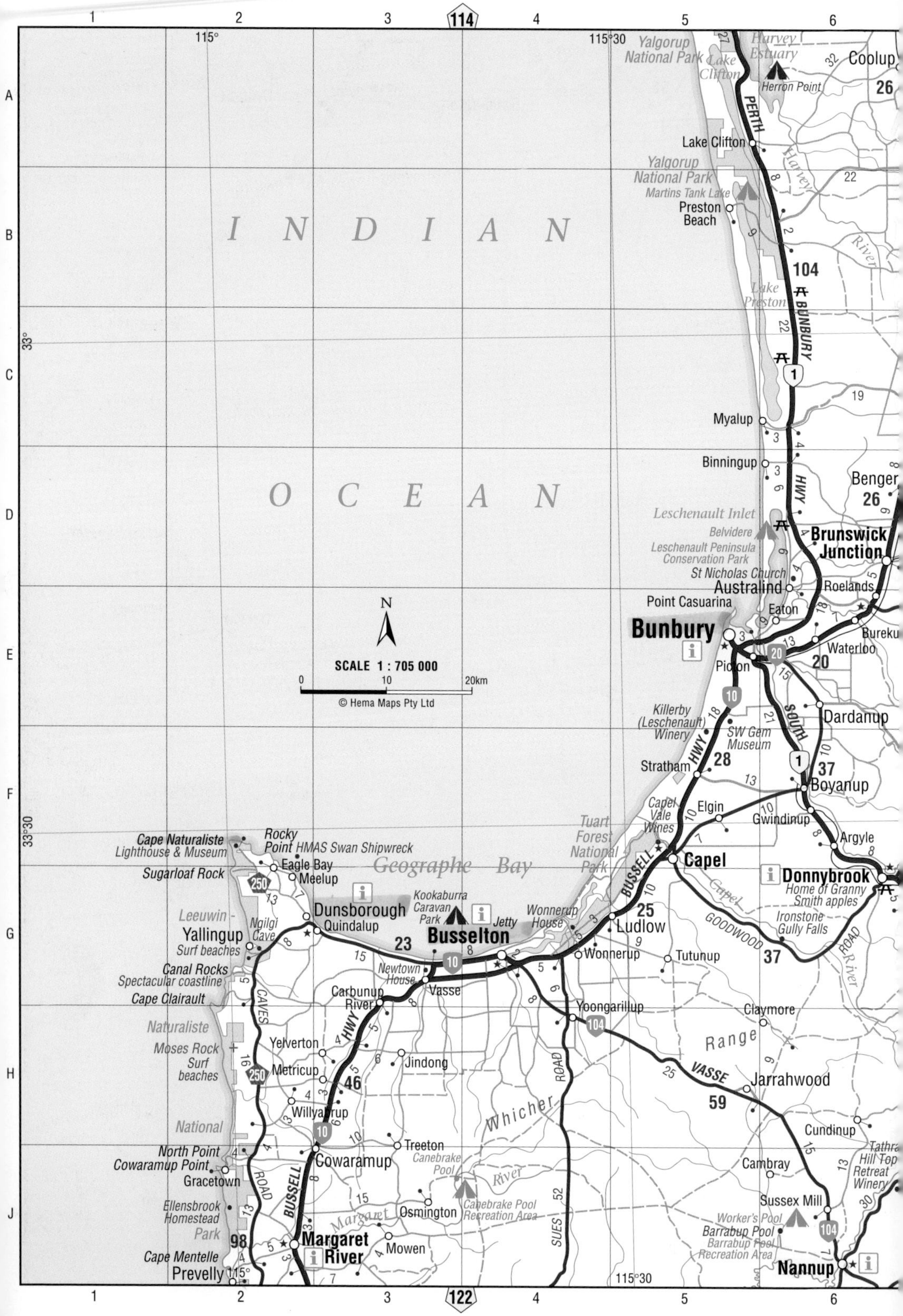

INDIAN OCEAN
SCALE 1 : 705 000
0 10 20km
© Hema Maps Pty Ltd
N
114
122
115°
115°30
33°
33°30
Yalgorup National Park
Lake Clifton
Harvey Estuary
Herron Point
Coolup
26
PERTH
Harvey
Lake Clifton
Yalgorup National Park
Martins Tank Lake
Preston Beach
22
River
104
Lake Preston
BUNBURY
1
19
Myalup
Binningup
HWY
Benger
26
Leschenault Inlet
Belvidere
Brunswick Junction
Leschenault Peninsula Conservation Park
St Nicholas Church
Australind
Roelands
Point Casuarina
Eaton
Bunbury
Bureku
Waterloo
20
Picton
10
Dardanup
Killerby (Leschenault) Winery
SW Gem Museum
SOUTH
Stratham
28
37
Boyanup
Elgin
Gwindinup
Capel Vale Wines
Tuart Forest National Park
Argyle
Capel
Donnybrook
Home of Granny Smith apples
Cape Naturaliste Lighthouse & Museum
Rocky Point
HMAS Swan Shipwreck
Eagle Bay
Meelup
Geographe Bay
Sugarloaf Rock
250
Dunsborough
Kookaburra Caravan Park
Jetty
Wonnerup House
BUSSELL
25
Ludlow
Ironstone Gully Falls
GOODWOOD
ROAD
Leeuwin-
Ngilgi Cave
Yallingup
Quindalup
Surf beaches
23
Busselton
Wonnerup
Tutunup
37
Canal Rocks
Spectacular coastline
Newtown House
Vasse
Cape Clairault
CAVES
Carbunup River
Yoongarillup
Claymore
Naturaliste
HWY
Range
Moses Rock
Surf beaches
Yelverton
Jindong
Metricup
46
ROAD
VASSE
Jarrahwood
59
Willyabrup
Whicher
National
Cundinup
North Point
Cowaramup Point
Treeton
Cowaramup
Canebrake Pool
River
Tathra Hill Top Retreat Winery
Gracetown
Cambray
Ellensbrook Homestead
Osmington
Canebrake Pool Recreation Area
Sussex Mill
Park
Margaret
SUES
Worker's Pool
Barrabup Pool
Barrabup Pool Recreation Area
98
Margaret River
Mowen
Cape Mentelle
Prevelly
Nannup

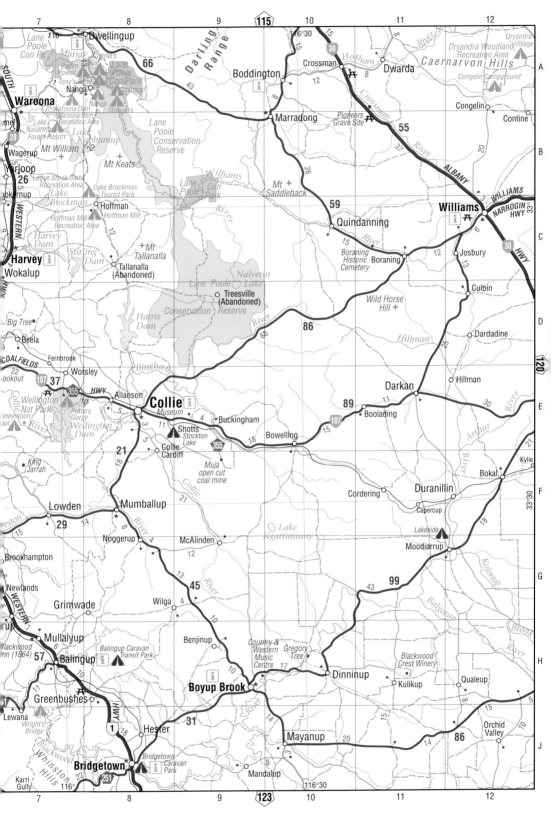

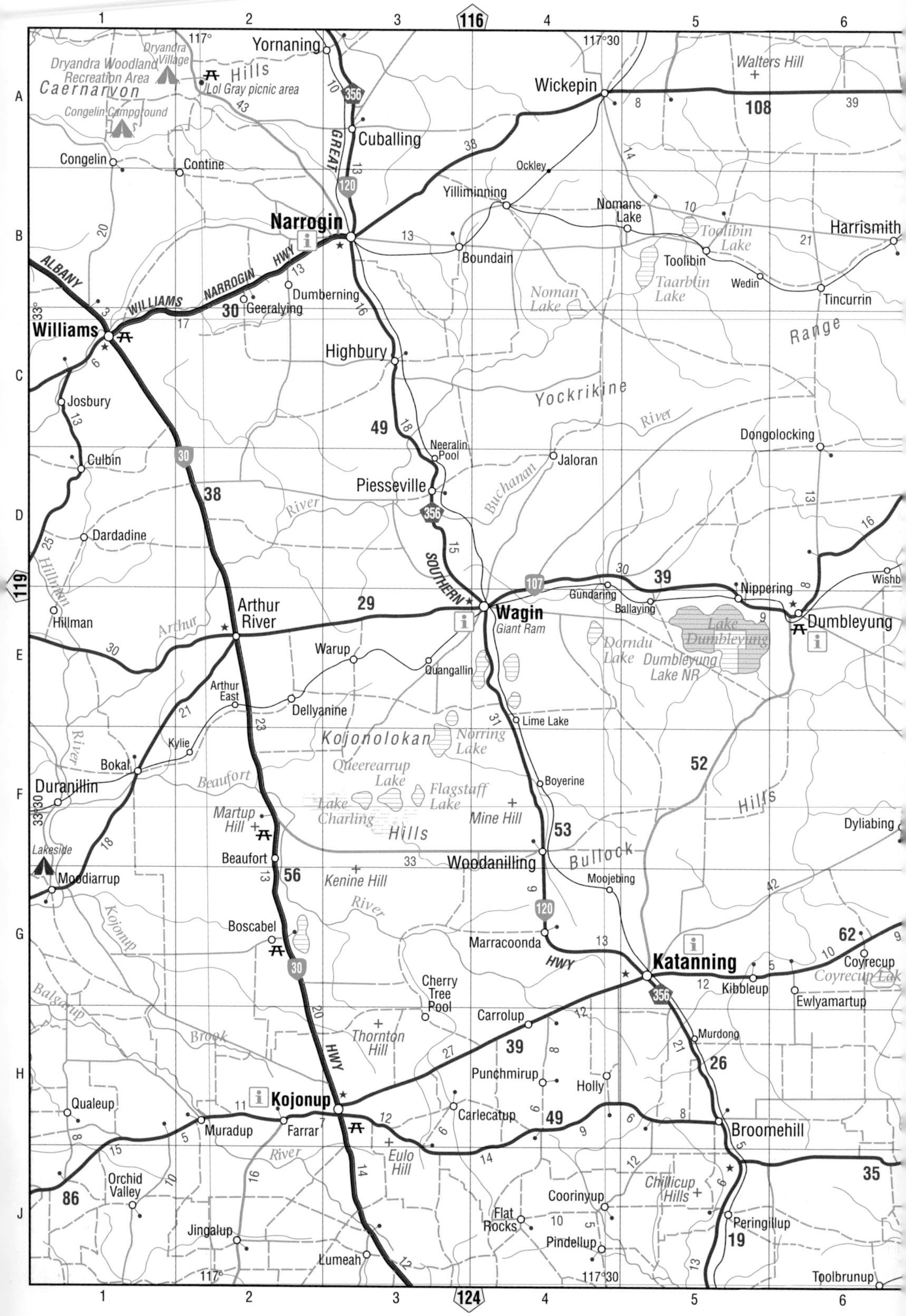

116

Yornaning
Dryandra Village
117°
Dryandra Woodland Recreation Area
Caernarvon Hills
Lol Gray picnic area
Congelin Campground
Wickepin
Walters Hill
117°30
108
39
8
Congelin
Contine
Cuballing
356
43
10
38
Ockley
14
Narrogin
Yilliminning
Nomans Lake
10
Toolibin Lake
Harrismith
120
13
Boundain
Toolibin
Taarblin Lake
21
Wedin
Geeralying
Dumberning
Noman Lake
Tincurrin
ALBANY
WILLIAMS
NARROGIN HWY
30
20
16
Williams
17
Highbury
Yockrikine
Range
Josbury
13
49
18
Neeralin Pool
Jaloran
Dongolocking
Culbin
30
38
Piesseville
Buchanan River
13
16
Dardadine
25
356
15
119
Hillman
SOUTHERN
30
39
Gundaring
Nippering
8
Wishb
Arthur River
29
Wagin
Giant Ram
Ballaying
9
Dumbleyung
30
107
Dorndu Lake
Lake Dumbleyung
Arthur East
21
Warup
Dumbleyung Lake NR
52
Dellyanine
23
Quangallin
Koljonolokan
Norring Lake
31
Lime Lake
Kylie
Queerearrup Lake
Boyerine
Dyliabing
Bokal
Beaufort
Flagstaff Lake
Mine Hill
53
Hills
Duranillin
Lake Charling
Hills
Bullock
42
33/30
Martup Hill
Beaufort
33
Woodanilling
Lakeside
18
13
56
Kenine Hill
River
120
Moojebing
Moodiarrup
Boscabel
9
13
62
30
Marracoonda
Katanning
10
Coyrecup
Kojonup
Balgarup
Cherry Tree Pool
HWY
356
12
Kibbleup
Coyrecup Lak
Carrolup
Ewlyamartup
20
Thornton Hill
27
12
Murdong
39
8
26
HWY
Punchmirup
21
Holly
Qualeup
11
Kojonup
Carlecatup
49
Broomehill
Muradup
Farrar
12
8
5
35
15
5
Eulo Hill
14
9
6
16
12
Coorinyup
Chillicup Hills
86
Orchid Valley
Flat Rocks
10
5
Peringillup
19
Jingalup
Pindellup
117°30
Lumeah
13
Toolbrunup
117°
124

120

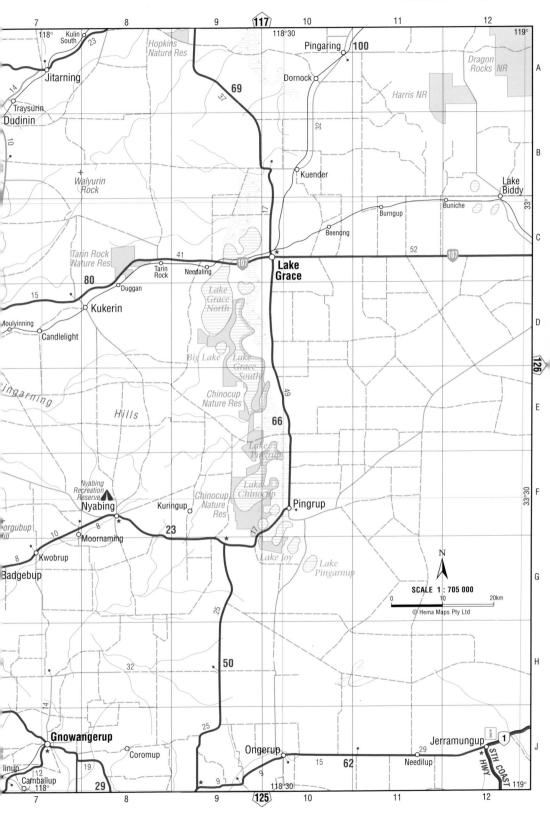

SCALE 1 : 705 000

0   10   20km

© Hema Maps Pty Ltd

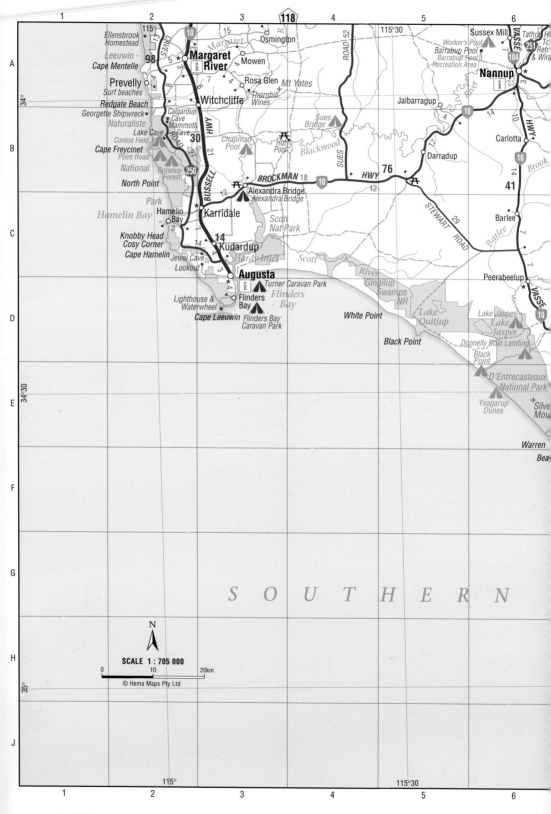

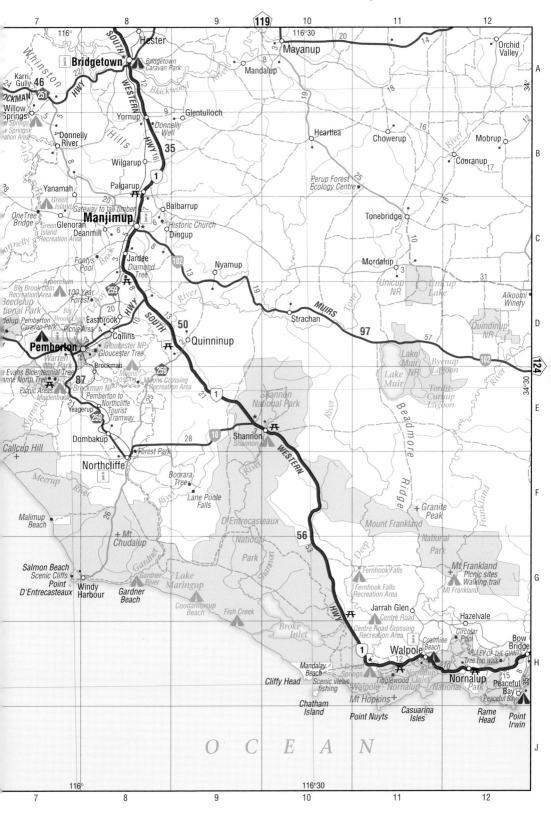

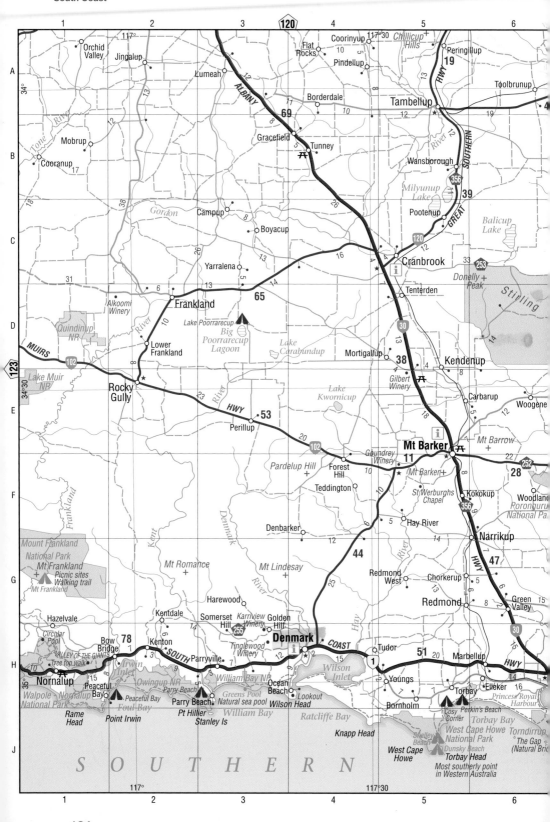

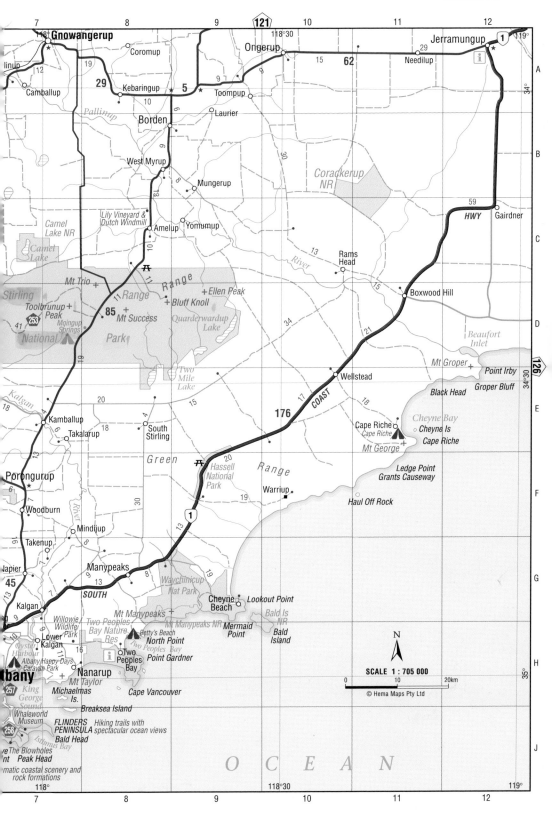

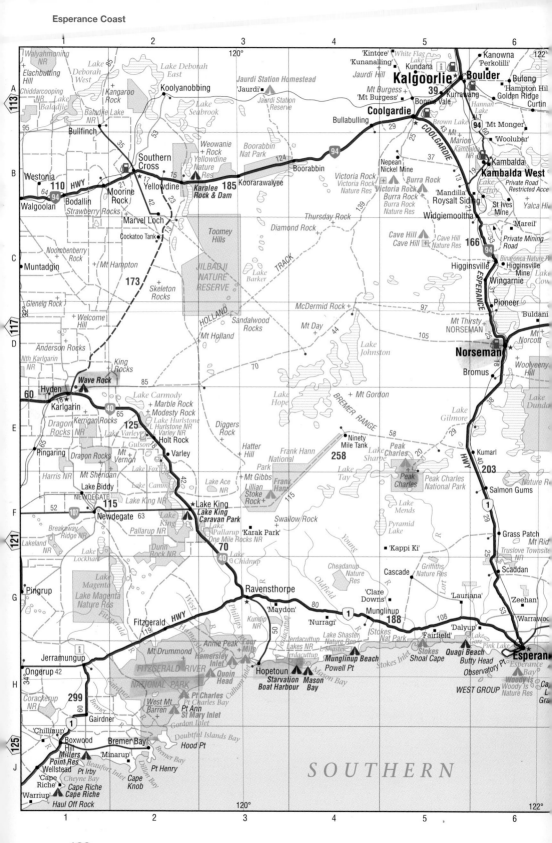

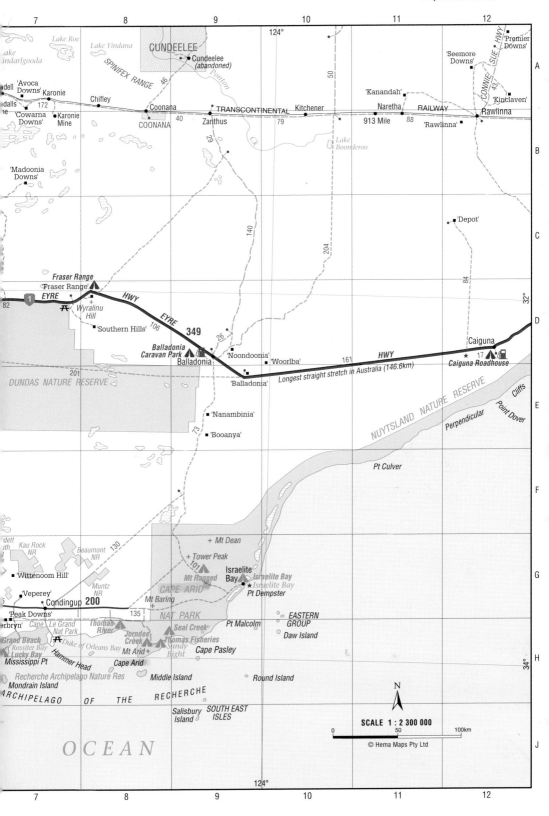

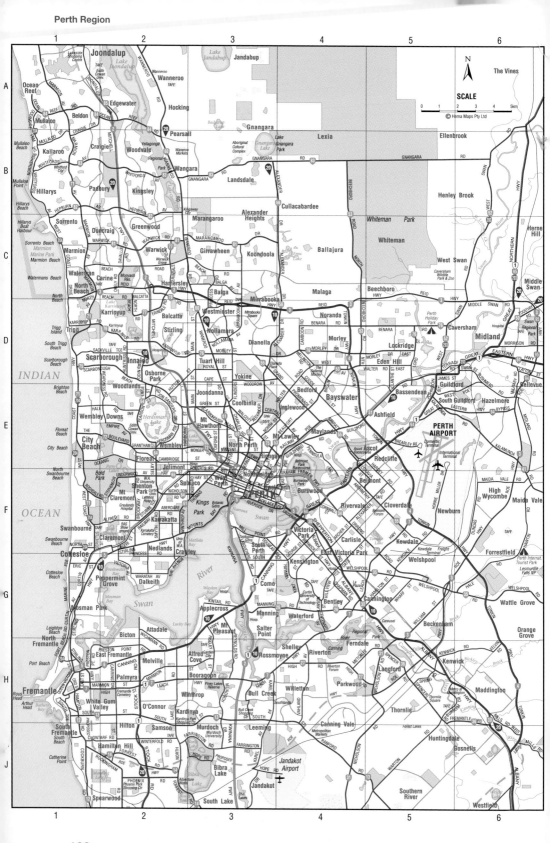